STAG LINES

The Anthology of
Virile Verse

Edited by
MAXWELL DROKE

MAXWELL DROKE, Publisher, INDIANAPOLIS

PRINTED IN THE UNITED STATES OF AMERICA

To the Messieurs Haig & Haig and the Walkers—Hiram and Johnnie — who have done much to stimulate the interest in virile verse.

"THEY HAD NO POET . . ."

"Vain was the chief's, the sage's pride!
  They had no poet and they died."—*Pope.*

By Tigris, or the streams of Ind,
  Ere Colchis rose, or Babylon,
Forgotten empires dreamed and sinned,
  Setting tall towns against the dawn,

Which, when the proud Sun smote upon,
  Flashed fire for fire and pride for pride;
Their names were . . . Ask oblivion! . . .
  "They had no poet, and they died."

Queens, dusk of hair and tawny-skinned,
  That loll where fellow leopards fawn . . .
Their hearts are dust before the wind,
  Their loves, that shook the world, are wan!

Passion is mighty . . . but, anon,
  Strong Death has Romance for his bride;
Their legends . . . Ask oblivion! . . .
  "They had no poet, and they died." . . .
            —Don Marquis.

ACKNOWLEDGMENTS

We express, in this formal way, our thanks to authors, agents, and publishers for permission to reprint copyrighted poems as follows:

BILL ADAMS—for *The Ballad of the Ivanhoe*.

GEORGE ADE—for *R-E-M-O-R-S-E*.

D. APPLETON-CENTURY COMPANY—for *The Woman Who Understands* from *The Quiet Courage*, by Everard Jack Appleton; *The Prairies* from the Poetical Works of William Cullen Bryant.

MRS. KATHERINE M. CARRUTH—for *Each in His Own Tongue* by Herbert Carruth.

ESTATE OF EDMUND VANCE COOKE—for *How Did You Die?* from *Impertinent Poems*.

DINGWALL-ROCK, LTD.—for *Inscription at The City of Brass*, from Arabian Nights, translated by Edward Powys Mathers.

DODD, MEAD & COMPANY—for *A Hymn*, by Gilbert Keith Chesterton; *A Ballad of a Nun*, by John Davidson.

DOUBLEDAY, DORAN & COMPANY—for *They Had No Poet* from *Dreams and Dust* by Don Marquis; *Gipsy Heart*, from *In Deep Places* by Amelia Josephine Burr.

E. P. DUTTON & COMPANY, INC.—for *Blessing on Little Boys* and *The Pioneer* from *I Sing The Pioneer* by Arthur Guiterman.

FUNK & WAGNALLS COMPANY—for *Life and Death* from *Swords & Ploughshares* by Ernest H. Crosby.

HAMLIN GARLAND—for *The Mountains Are a Lonely Folk* and *Do You Fear The Force of the Wind?*

HARCOURT, BRACE & COMPANY—for *Caliban in the Coal Mines* from Selected Poems of Louis Untermeyer.

HENRY HOLT & COMPANY—for *Prayers of Steel* from *Corn-huskers* by Carl Sandburg; *The Little Ships That Never Sail* by Glenn Ward Dresbach.

HOUGHTON, MIFFLIN & COMPANY—for *Out Where the West Begins* by Arthur Chapman.

THE JAQUA COMPANY—for *The Prayer of an Outdoor Man* by Wilfred A. Peterson.

KALEIDOGRAPH PRESS—for *Earth Victory* by Lewis Morgan.

MITCHELL KENNERLEY, PUBLISHER—for *They Went Forth to Battle but They Always Fell,* by Shaemas O'Sheel.

ROBERT W. KERNAGHAN—for *The Stay-at-Homes.*

S. E. KISER—for *The Fighter.*

ALFRED A. KNOPF, INC.—for *The Slave* by James Oppenheim; *Ghost* by John V. A. Weaver.

THE MACMILLAN COMPANY—for *The Ghosts of the Buffaloes* by Vachel Lindsay; *The Yarn of the 'Nancy Bell'* by W. S. Gilbert.

ESTATE OF DOUGLAS MALLOCH—for *Today.*

MISS JUANITA MILLER—for *Columbus* by Joaquin Miller.

DAVID MORTON—for *Lover to Lover.*

ESTATE OF JOHN BOYLE O'REILLY—for *The Cry of the Dreamer.*

PINKER & MORRISON, AGENTS—for *Prayer* and *A Phantasy of Heaven,* by Harry Kemp.

BARTON REES POGUE—for *Beau Night* and *I Wish I Could Learn to Laugh at Myself.*

THE REILLY & LEE COMPANY—for *It Couldn't be Done,* by Edgar A. Guest.

GEORGE ROUTLEDGE & SONS, LTD.—for *Rosy Wine,* by W. J. Linton.

CHARLES SCRIBNER'S SONS—for *I Have a Rendezvous With Death,* by Alan Seeger; *John Evereldown,* by Edwin Arlington Robinson and *When Trout Swim Down Great Ormond Street,* by Conrad Aiken.

MRS. FRANK L. STANTON—for *A Poor Unfortunate,* by Frank L. Stanton.

TRAMP STARR—for *Farm Funeral.*

FREDERICK A. STOKES COMPANY—for *The Highwayman,* from the Collected Poems of Alfred Noyes.

THE VIKING PRESS—for *Ballade of Unfortunate Mammals,* from *Not So Deep as a Well,* by Dorothy Parker.

CONTENTS

I

THE STAG AND EVE

"So the clouds may come and the rain may fall,
   The shadows may creep and the dead men crawl,—
   But I follow the women wherever they call,
      And that's why I'm going to Tilbury Town."

— *"John Evereldown" by*
Edwin Arlington Robinson

TO HIS COY MISTRESS

Had we but world enough, and time,
This coyness, lady, were no crime.
We would sit down, and think which way
To walk, and pass our long love's day.
Thou by the Indian Ganges' side
Shouldst rubies find: I by the tide
Of Humber would complain. I would
Love you ten years before the flood,
And you should, if you please, refuse
Till the conversion of the Jews;
My vegetable love should grow
Vaster than empires and more slow;
An hundred years should go to praise
Thine eyes, and on thy forehead gaze;
Two hundred to adore each breast,
But thirty thousand to the rest;
An age at least to every part,
And the last age should show your heart.
For, lady, you deserve this state,
Nor would I love at lower rate.
　　But at my back I always hear
Time's wingèd chariot hurrying near,
And yonder all before us lie
Deserts of vast eternity.
Thy beauty shall no more be found,
Nor, in thy marble vault, shall sound
My echoing song; then worms shall try
That long-preserved virginity,
And your quaint honour turn to dust,
And into ashes all my lust:
The grave's a fine and private place,

But none, I think, do there embrace.
  Now therefore, while the youthful hue
Sits on thy skin like morning dew,
And while thy willing soul transpires
At every pore with instant fires,
Now let us sport us while we may,
And now, like amorous birds of prey,
Rather at once our time devour,
Than languish in his slow-chapt power,
Let us roll all our strength and all
Our sweetness up into one ball,
And tear our pleasures with rough strife
Through the iron gates of life;
Thus, though we cannot make our sun
Stand still, yet we will make him run.
                    —*Andrew Marvell.*

2

THE TIME I'VE LOST IN WOOING

The time I've lost in wooing,
In watching and pursuing
    The light that lies
    In woman's eyes,
Has been my heart's undoing.
Tho' Wisdom oft has sought me,
I scorn'd the lore she brought me,
    My only books
    Were woman's looks,
And folly's all they taught me.

Her smile when Beauty granted,
I hung with gaze enchanted,

Like him the Sprite
Whom maids by night
Oft meet in glen that's haunted.
Like him, too, Beauty won me;
If once their ray
Was turn'd away,
O! winds could not outrun me.

And are those follies going?
And is my proud heart growing
Too cold or wise
For brilliant eyes
Again to set it glowing?
No—vain, alas! th' endeavour
From bonds so sweet to sever;—
Poor Wisdom's chance
Against a glance
Is now as weak as ever.

—*Thomas Moore.*

3

A DIRGE

Ring out your bells, let mourning shews be spread;
For Love is dead:
All Love is dead, infected
With plague of deep disdain:
Worth, as nought worth, rejected,
And Faith fair scorn doth gain.
From so ungrateful fancy
From such a female frenzy,
From them that use men thus,
Good Lord, deliver us!

Weep, neighbours, weep do you not hear it said
That Love is dead?
   His death-bed, peacock's folly;
His winding-sheet is shame;
   His will, false-seeming wholly;
His sole executor, blame.
   From so ungrateful fancy,
   From such a female frenzy,
   From them that use men thus,
   Good Lord, deliver us!

Let dirge be sung, and trentals rightly read,
For Love is dead;
   Sir Wrong his tomb ordaineth
My mistress' marble heart;
   Which epitaph containeth,
"Her eyes were once his dart."
   From so ungrateful fancy,
   From such a female frenzy,
   From them that use men thus,
   Good Lord, deliver us!

Alas, I lie: rage hath this error bred;
Love is not dead;
   Love is not dead, but sleepeth
In her unmatchèd mind,
   Where she his counsel keepeth,
Till due deserts she find.
   Therefore from so vile fancy,
   To call such wit a frenzy,
   Who Love can temper thus,
   Good Lord, deliver us!

—*Sir Philip Sidney.*

4

SHALL I, WASTING IN DESPAIR

Shall I, wasting in despair,
Die because a woman's fair?
Or make pale my cheeks with care
'Cause another's rosy are?
Be she fairer than the day,
Or the flowery meads in May,
　If she be not so to me
　What care I how fair she be?

Should my heart be grieved or pined
'Cause I see a woman kind?
Or a well-disposèd nature
Joinèd with a lovely feature?
Be she meeker, kinder than
Turtle-dove, or pelican,
　If she be not so to me,
　What care I how kind she be?

Shall a woman's virtues move
Me to perish for her love?
Or her well-deserving, known,
Make me quite forget my own?
Be she with that goodness blest
Which may gain her name of best,
　If she be not such to me
　What care I how good she be?

'Cause her fortune seems too high,
Shall I play the fool, and die?
Those that bear a noble mind,
Where they want of riches find,

Think what with them they would do
That without them dare to woo;
   And unless that mind I see,
   What care I though great she be?

Great, or good, or kind, or fair,
I will ne'er the more despair:
If she love me, this believe
I will die ere she shall grieve:
If she slight me when I woo,
I can scorn and let her go;
   For if she be not for me,
   What care I for whom she be?
               —*George Wither.*

5

DELIGHT IN DISORDER

A sweet disorder in the dress
Kindles in clothes a wantonness;
A lawn about the shoulders thrown
Into a fine distraction;
An erring lace, which here and there
Enthrals a crimson stomacher;
A cuff neglectful, and thereby
Ribands to flow confusedly;
A winning wave, deserving note,
In the tempestuous petticoat;
A careless shoe-string, in whose tie
I see a wild civility;
Do more bewitch me, than when art
Is too precise in every part.
               —*Robert Herrick.*

6

WISHES FOR THE SUPPOSED MISTRESS

Whoe'er she be,
That not impossible She
That shall command my heart and me;

Where'er she lie,
Lock'd up from mortal eye
In shady leaves of destiny:

Till that ripe birth
Of studied Fate stand forth,
And teach her fair steps tread our earth

Till that divine
Idea take a shrine
Of crystal flesh, through which to shine:

—Meet you her, my Wishes,
Bespeak her to my blisses,
And be ye call'd, my absent kisses.

I wish her beauty
That owes not all its duty
To gaudy tire, or glist'ring shoe-tie:

Something more than
Taffata or tissue can,
Or rampant feather, or rich fan.

A face that's best
By its own beauty drest,
And can alone commend the rest:

A face made up
Out of no other shop
That what Nature's white hand sets ope.

Sydneian showers
Of sweet discourse, whose powers
Can crown old Winter's head with flowers.

Whate'er delight
Can make day's forehead bright
Or give down to the wings of night.

Soft silken hours,
Open suns, shady bowers;
'Bove all, nothing within that lowers.

Days, that need borrow
No part of their good morrow
From a fore-spent night of sorrow:

Days, that in spite
Of darkness, by the light
Of a clear mind are day all night.

Life, that dares send
A challenge to his end,
And when it comes, say, "Welcome, friend."

I wish her store
Of worth may leave her poor
Of wishes; and I wish—no more.

—Now, if Time knows
That Her, whose radiant brows
Weave them a garland of my vows;

Her that dares be
What these lines wish to see:
I seek no further, it is She.

'Tis She, and here
Lo! I unclothe and clear
My wishes' cloudy character.

Such worth as this is
Shall fix my flying wishes,
And determine them to kisses.

Let her full glory
My fancies, fly before ye;
Be ye my fictions:—but her story.

—*R. Crashaw.*

7

HOW CAN YE BLUME SAE FAIR?

Ye banks and braes o' bonnie Doon,
   How can ye blume sae fair!
How can ye chant, ye little birds,
   And I saw fu' o' care!

Thou'll break my heart, thou bonnie bird
   That sings upon the bough;
Thou minds me o' the happy days
   When my fause Luve was true.

Thou'll break my heart, thou bonnie bird
   That sings beside thy mate;
For sae I sat, and sae I sang,
   And wist na o' my fate.

Aft hae I roved by bonnie Doon
   To see the woodbine twine,
And ilka bird sang o' its love;
   And sae did I o' mine.

Wi' lightsome heart I pu'd a rose,
   Frae aff its thorny tree;
And my fause luver staw the rose,
   But left the thorn wi' me.

                      —*Robert Burns.*

8

FREEDOM AND LOVE

How delicious is the winning
Of a kiss at love's beginning,
When two mutual hearts are sighing
For the knot there's no untying!

Yet remember, 'midst your wooing
Love has bliss, but Love has ruing;
Other smiles may make you fickle,
Tears for other charms may trickle.

Love he comes and Love he tarries
Just as fate or fancy carries;
Longest stays, when sorest chidden;
Laughs and flies, when press'd and bidden.

Bind the sea to slumber stilly,
Bind its odor to the lily,
Bind the aspen ne'er to quiver,
Then bind Love to last for ever.

Love's a fire that needs renewal
Of fresh beauty for its fuel:
Love's wing moults when caged and captured,
Only free, he soars enraptured.

Can you keep the bee from ranging,
Or the ringdove's neck from changing?
No! nor fetter'd Love from dying
In the knot there's no untying.

                              —*J. Campbell.*

9

SIMPLEX MUNDITIIS

Still to be neat, still to be dressed
As you were going to a feast;
Still to be powdered, still perfumed:
Lady, it is to be presumed,
Though art's hid causes are not found,
All is not sweet, all is not sound.

Give me a look, give me a face,
That makes simplicity a grace;
Robes loosely flowing, hair as free:
Such sweet neglect more taketh me
Than all the adulteries of art;
They strike mine eyes, but not my heart.

                              —*Ben Jonson.*

10

THE UNFAITHFUL SHEPHERDESS

While that the sun with his beams hot
Scorchéd the fruits in vale and mountain,
Philon the shepherd, late forgot,
Sitting beside a crystal fountain,
   In shadow of a green oak tree
   Upon his pipe this song play'd he:
Adieu Love, adieu Love, untrue Love;
Untrue Love, untrue Love, adieu Love;
Your mind is light, soon lost for new love.

So long as I was in your sight
I was your heart, your soul, and treasure;
And evermore you sobb'd and sigh'd
Burning in flames beyond all measure:
   —Three days endured your love to me,
   And it was lost in other three!
Adieu Love, adieu Love, untrue Love,
Untrue Love, untrue Love, adieu Love;
Your mind is light, soon lost for new love.

Another Shepherd you did see
To whom your heart was soon enchainéd;
Full soon your love was leapt from me,
Full soon my place he had obtainéd.
   Soon came a third, your love to win,
   And we were out and he was in.
Adieu Love, adieu Love, untrue Love,
Untrue Love, untrue Love, adieu Love;
Your mind is light, soon lost for new love.

Sure you have made me passing glad
That you your mind so soon removéd,

Before that I the leisure had
To choose you for my best belovéd:
  For all your love was past and done
  Two days before it was begun:—
Adieu Love, adieu Love, untrue Love,
Untrue Love, untrue Love, adieu Love;
Your mind is light, soon lost for new love.

               —Anonymous.

11

THE INDIFFERENT

Never more will I protest
To love a woman, but in jest;
For as they can not be true,
So, to give each man his due,
  When the wooing fit is past
  Their affection cannot last.

Therefore, if I chance to meet
With a mistress fair and sweet,
She my service shall obtain,
Loving her for love again:
  Thus much liberty I crave,
  Not to be a constant slave.

But when we have tried each other,
If she better like another,
Let her quickly change for me;
Then to change am I as free.
  He or she that loves too long
  Sell their freedom for a song.

           —Francis Beaumont.

12

ON A GIRDLE

That which her slender waist confined
Shall now my joyful temples bind;
No monarch but would give his crown
His arms might do what this has done.

It was my Heaven's extremest sphere,
The pale which held that lovely deer:
My joy, my grief, my hope, my love,
Did all within this circle move.

A narrow compass! and yet there
Dwelt all that's good, and all that's fair!
Give me but what this ribband bound,
Take all the rest the sun goes round!
—*Edmund Waller.*

13

THE GIFT

Say, cruel Iris, pretty rake,
Dear mercenary beauty,
What annual offering shall I make,
Expressive of my duty?

My heart, a victim to thine eyes,
Should I at once deliver,
Say, would the angry fair one prize
The gift, who slights the giver?

A bill, a jewel, watch, or toy,
My rivals give—and let 'em;
If gems, or gold, impart a joy,
I'll give them—when I get 'em.

I'll give—but not the full-blown rose,
Or rose-bud more in fashion;
Such short-liv'd efferings but disclose
A transitory passion.

I'll give thee something yet unpaid,
Not less sincere, than civil:
I'll give thee—Ah! too charming maid,
I'll give thee—To the devil.
                    —*Oliver Goldsmith.*

14

OUT OF SIGHT, OUT OF MIND

The oftener seen, the more I lust,
The more I lust, the more I smart,
The more I smart, the more I trust,
The more I trust the heavier heart,
The heavy heart breeds mine unrest,
Thy absence therefore like I best.

The rarer seen, the less in mind,
The less in mind, the lesser pain,
The lesser pain, less grief I find,
The lesser grief, the greater gain,
The greater gain, the merrier I,
Therefore I wish thy sight to fly.

The further off, the more I joy,
The more I joy, the happier life,
The happier life less hurts annoy,
The lesser hurts, pleasure most rife,
Such pleasures rife shall I obtain
When distance doth depart us twain.
                    —*Barnabe Googe.*

15

COUNSEL TO GIRLS

Gather ye rose-buds while ye may,
    Old Time is still a-flying:
And this same flower that smiles to-day,
    To-morrow will be dying.

The glorious Lamp of Heaven, the Sun,
    The higher he's a-getting
The sooner will his race be run,
    And nearer he's to setting.

That age is best which is the first,
    When youth and blood are warmer;
But being spent, the worse, and worst
    Times, still succeed the former.

Then be not coy, but use your time;
    And while ye may, go marry:
For having lost but once your prime,
    You may for ever tarry.
                    —*Robert Herrick.*

16

WHEN THOU MUST HOME

When thou must home to shades of underground,
And there arrived, a new admired guest,
The beauteous spirits do engirt thee round,
White Iope, blithe Helen, and the rest,
To hear the stories of thy finished love
From that smooth tongue whose music hell can move.

Then wilt thou speak of banqueting delights,
Of masques and revels which sweet youth did make,
Of tourneys and great challenges of knights,
And all these triumphs for thy beauty's sake:
When thou hast told these honours done to thee,
Then tell, O tell, how thou didst murder me.

—Thomas Campion.

17

INSPIRATION

I never drank of Aganippe well,
Nor ever did in shade of Tempe sit,
And Muses scorn with vulgar brains to dwell;
Poor layman I, for sacred rites unfit.
Some do I hear of poets' fury tell,
But, God wot, wot not what they mean by it;
And this I swear by blackest brook of hell,
I am no pick-purse of another's wit.
How falls it then, that with so smooth an ease
My thoughts I speak; and what I speak doth flow
In verse, and that my verse best wits doth please?

Guess we the cause! What, is it thus? Fie, no.
Or so? Much less. How then? Sure thus it is,
My lips are sweet, inspired with Stella's kiss.
                              —*Sir Philip Sidney.*

18

LYING

I do confess, in many a sigh,
My lips have breath'd you many a lie,
And who, with such delights in view,
Would lose them for a lie or two?

Nay—look not thus, with brow reproving:
Lies are, my dear, the soul of loving!
If half we tell the girls were true,
If half we swear to think and do,
Were aught but lying's bright illusion,
The world would be in strange confusion!
If ladies' eyes were, every one,
As lovers swear, a radiant sun,
Astronomy should leave the skies,
To learn her lore in ladies' eyes!
Oh no!—believe me, lovely girl,
When nature turns your teeth to pearl,
Your neck to snow, your eyes to fire,
Your yellow locks to golden wire,
Then, only then, can heaven decree,
That you should live for only me,
Or I for you, as night and morn,
We've swearing kiss'd, and kissing sworn.
And now, my gentle hints to clear,
For once, I'll tell you truth, my dear!

Whenever you may chance to meet
A loving youth, whose love is sweet,
Long as you're false and he believes you,
Long as you trust and he deceives you,
So long the blissful bond endures;
And while he lies, his heart is yours:
But, oh! you've wholly lost the youth
The instant that he tells you truth!
                              —*Thomas Moore.*

19

THE FEMALE OF THE SPECIES

When the Himalayan peasant meets the he-bear in his pride,
He shouts to scare the monster, who will often turn aside.
But the she-bear thus accosted rends the peasant tooth and
    nail.
For the female of the species is more deadly than the male.

When Nag the basking cobra hears the careless foot of man,
He will sometimes wriggle sideways and avoid it if he can.
But his mate makes no such motion where she camps beside
    the trail.
For the female of the species is more deadly than the male.

When the early Jesuit fathers preached to Hurons and
    Choctaws,
They prayed to be delivered from the vengeance of the
    squaws.
'Twas the women, not the warriors, turned those stark en-
    thusiasts pale.
For the female of the species is more deadly than the male.

Man's timid heart is bursting with the things he must not say,
For the Woman that God gave him isn't his to give away;
But when hunter meets with husband, each confirms the
other's tale—
The female of the species is more deadly than the male.

Man, a bear in most relations—worm and savage otherwise,—
Man propounds negotiations, Man accepts the compromise.
Very rarely will he squarely push the logic of a fact
To its ultimate conclusion in unmitigated act.

Fear, or foolishness, impels him, ere he lay the wicked low,
To concede some form of trial even to his fiercest foe.
Mirth obscene diverts his anger—Doubt and Pity oft perplex
Him in dealing with an issue—to the scandal of The Sex!

But the Woman that God gave him, every fibre of her frame
Proves her launched for one sole issue, armed and engined
for the same;
And to serve that single issue, lest the generations fail,
The female of the species must be deadlier than the male.

She who faces Death by torture for each life beneath her
breast
May not deal in doubt or pity—must not swerve for fact or
jest.
These be purely male diversions—not in these her honour
dwells.
She the Other Law we live by, is that Law and nothing else.

She can bring no more to living than the powers that make
her great
As the Mother of the Infant and the Mistress of the Mate.
And when Babe and Man are lacking and she strides un-
claimed to claim
Her right as femme (and baron), her equipment is the same.

She is wedded to convictions—in default of grosser ties:
Her contentions are her children, Heaven help him who
 denies!—
He will meet no suave discussion, but the instant, white-hot,
 wile,
Wakened female of the species warring as for spouse and
 child.

Unprovoked and awful charges—even so the she-bear fights,
Speech that drips, corrodes, and poisons—even so the cobra
 bites,
Scientific vivisection of one nerve till it is raw
And the victim writhes in anguish—like the Jesuit with the
 squaw!

So it comes that Man, the coward, when he gathers to confer
With his fellow-braves in council, dare not leave a place for
 her
Where, at war with Life and Conscience, he uplifts his erring
 hands
To Some God of Abstract Justice—which no woman understands.

And Man knows it! Knows, moreover, that the Woman that
 God gave him
Must command but may not govern—shall enthrall but not
 enslave him.
And *She* knows, because She warns him, and Her instincts
 never fail,
That the Female of Her Species is more deadly than the Male.
                                   —*Rudyard Kipling.*

20
THE LADIES

I've taken my fun where I've found it;
I've rouged an' I've ranged in my time;
I've 'ad my pickin' o' sweethearts,
An' four o' the lot was prime.
One was an 'art-caste widow,
One was a woman at Prome,
One was the wife of a jemadar-sais, (head-groom)
An' one is a girl at 'ome.

> *Now I aren't no 'and with the ladies,*
> *For, takin' 'em all along,*
> *You never can say till you've tried 'em,*
> *An' then you are like to be wrong.*
> *There's times when you'll think that you mightn't,*
> *There's times when you'll know that you might;*
> *But the things you will learn from the Yellow an'*
>   *Brown,*
> *They'll 'elp you a lot with the White!*

I was a young un at 'Oogli,
Shy as a girl to begin;
Aggie de Castrer she made me,
An' Aggie was clever as sin;
Older than me, but my first un—
More like a mother she were—
Showed me the way to promotion an' pay,
An' I learned about women from 'er!

Then I was ordered to Burma,
Actin' in charge o' Bazar,
An' I got me a tiddy live 'eathen
Through buyin' supplies off 'er pa.

Funny an' yellow an' faithful—
Doll in a teacup she were—
But we lived on the square, like a true-married pair,
An' I learned about women from 'er!

Then we was shifted to Neemuch
(Or I might ha' been keepin' 'er now),
An' I took with a shiny she-devil,
The wife a nigger at Mhow;
'Taught me the gipsy-folks' *bolee;* (slang)
Kind o' volcano she were,
For she knifed me one night 'cause I wished she was
      white,
And I learned about women from 'er!

Then I come 'ome in a trooper,
'Long of a kid o' sixteen—
'Girl from a convent at Meerut,
The straightest I ever 'ave seen.
Love at first sight was 'er trouble,
She didn't know what it were;
An' I wouldn't do such, 'cause I like 'er too much,
But—I learned about women from 'er!

I've taken my fun where I've found it,
An' now I must pay for my fun,
For the more you 'ave know o' the others
The less will you settle to one;
An' the end of it's sittin' and thinkin',
An' dreamin' Hell-fires to see;
So be warned by my lot (which I know you will not),
An' learn about women from me!

                 —*Rudyard Kipling.*

21

A SONG OF IMPOSSIBILITIES

Lady, I loved you all last year,
  How honestly and well—
Alas! would weary you to hear,
  And torture me to tell;
I raved beneath the midnight sky,
  I sang beneath the limes—
Orlando in my lunacy,
  And Petrarch in my rhymes.
But all is over! When the sun
  Dries up the boundless main,
When black is white, false-hearted one,
  I may be yours again!

When passion's early hopes and fears
  Are not derided things;
When truth is found in falling tears,
  Or faith in golden rings;
When the dark Fates that rule our way
  Instruct me where they hid
One woman that would ne'er betray,
  One friend that never lied;
When summer shines without a cloud,
  And bliss without a pain;
When worth is noticed in a crowd,
  I may be yours again!

.   .   .

When you can cancel what has been,
  Or alter what must be,
Or bring once more that vanished scene,
  Those withered joys to me;

When you can tune the broken lute,
 Or deck the blighted wreath,
Or rear the garden's richest fruit,
 Upon a blasted heath;
When you can lure the wolf at bay
 Back to his shattered chain,
To-day may then be yesterday—
 I may be yours again!
  —*Winthrop Mackworth Praed.*

22

SYMPATHY

A knight and a lady once met in a grove
While each was in quest of a fugitive love;
A river ran mournfully murmuring by,
And they wept in its waters for sympathy.

"Oh, never was knight such a sorrow that bore!"
"Oh, never was maid so deserted before!"
"From life and its woes let us instantly fly,
And jump in together for company!"

They searched for an eddy that suited the deed,
But here was a bramble and there was a weed;
"How tiresome it is!" said the fair, with a sigh;
So they sat down to rest them in company.

They gazed at each other, the maid and the knight;
How fair was her form, and how goodly his height!
"One mournful embrace," sobbed the youth, "ere
    we die!"
So kissing and crying kept company.

"Oh, had I but loved such an angel as you!"
"Oh, had but my swain been a quarter as true!"
"To miss such perfection how blinded was I!"
Sure now they were excellent company!

At length spoke the lass, 'twixt a smile and a tear,
"The weather is cold for a watery bier;
When summer returns we may easily die,
Till then let us sorrow in company."

—*Reginald Heber.*

23

THE BACHELOR'S DREAM

My pipe is lit, my grog is mixed,
My curtains drawn and all is snug;
Old Puss is in her elbow-chair,
And Tray is sitting on the rug.
Last night I had a curious dream,
Miss Susan Bates was Mistress Mogg—
What d'ye think of that, my cat?
What d'ye think of that, my dog?

She looked so fair, she sang so well,
I could but woo and she was won;
Myself in blue, the bride in white,
The ring was placed, the deed was done!
Away we went in chaise-and-four,
As fast as grinning boys could flog—
What d'ye think of that, my cat?
What d'ye think of that, my dog?

At times we had a spar, and then
Mama must mingle in the song—

The sister took a sister's part—
The maid declared her master wrong—
The parrot learned to call me "Fool!"
My life was like a London fog—
What d'ye think of that, my cat?
What d'ye think of that, my dog?

My Susan's taste was superfine,
As proved by bills that had no end;
I never had a decent coat—
I never had a coin to spend!
She forced me to resign my club,
Lay down my pipe, retrench my grog—
What d'ye think of that, my cat?
What d'ye think of that, my dog?

Each Sunday night we gave a rout
To fops and flirts, a pretty list;
And when I tried to steal away,
I found my study full of whist!
Then, first to come, and last to go,
There always was a Captain Hogg—
What d'ye think of that, my cat?
What d'ye think of that, my dog?

Now was not that an awful dream
For one who single is and snug—
With Pussy in the elbow-chair,
And Tray reposing on the rug?—
If I must totter down the hill,
'Tis safest done without a clog—
What d'ye think of that, my cat?
What d'ye think of that, my dog?

     —*Thomas Hood.*

24

THE DIFFERENCE DEFINED

"I can't conceive" she archly cried,
"Wherein you men can longer pride
   Yourselves from female rivals free.
   For surely we have grown to be
Your peers in ev'ry human stride.
It is a truth that none dare hide;
   Yet why you men will not agree
   To recognize the new decree
           I can't conceive.

"Now, *entre nous,* wont you confide
And tell me true, all jokes aside,
   What difference the world can see
   Between your manly self and me?
"To tell you truly," he replied,
           "I can't conceive"
           —*Anonymous.*

25

SALLY IN OUR ALLEY

Of all the girls that are so smart
   There's none like pretty Sally;
She is the darling of my heart,
   And she lives in our alley.
There is no lady in the land
   Is half so sweet as Sally;
She is the darling of my heart,
   And she lives in our alley.

Her father he makes cabbage-nets
   And through the streets does cry 'em;
Her mother she sells laces long
   To such as please to buy 'em:
But sure such folks could ne'er beget
   So sweet a girl as Sally!
She is the darling of my heart,
   And she lives in our alley.

When she is by, I leave my work,
   I love her so sincerely;
My master comes like any Turk,
   And bangs me most severely—
But let him bang his bellyful,
   I'll bear it all for Sally;
She is the darling of my heart,
   And she lives in our alley.

Of all the days that's in the week
   I dearly love but one day—
And that's the day that comes betwixt
   A Saturday and Monday;
For then I'm drest all in my best
   To walk abroad with Sally.
She is the darling of my heart,
   And she lives in our alley.

My master carries me to church,
   And often am I blamed
Because I leave him in the lurch
   As soon as text is named;
I leave the church in sermon-time
   And slink away to Sally;
She is the darling of my heart,
   And she lives in our alley.

When Christmas comes about again
  O then I shall have money;
I'll hoard it up, and box it all,
  I'll give it to my honey;
I would it were ten thousand pound,
  I'd give it all to Sally;
She is the darling of my heart,
  And she lives in our alley.

My master and the neighbors all
  Make game of me and Sally,
And, but for her, I'd better be
  A slave and row a galley;
But when my seven long years are out
  O then I'll marry Sally,—
O then we'll wed, and then we'll bed,
  But not in our alley!

                    —*H. Carey.*

26

BEAUTY

Horns to bulls wise Nature lends;
Horses she with hoofs defends;
Hares with nimble feet relieves;
Dreadful teeth to lions gives;
Fishes learn through streams to slide;
Birds through yielding air to glide;
Men with courage she supplies;
But to women these denies.
What then gives she? Beauty, this

Both their arms and armor is:
She, that can this weapon use,
Fire and sword with ease subdues.
—*Thomas Stanley.*

27

ON HER DANCING

I stood and saw my Mistress dance,
Silent, and with so fixed an eye,
Some might suppose me in a trance:
   But being asked why,
By one who knew I was in love,
   I could not but impart
My wonder, to behold her move
So nimbly with a marble heart.
—*James Shirley.*

28

COUNT A HUNDRED

If her eyes are softly lighted, like the moonlight on the moors;
If she moves a little closer, puts her little hand in yours,
Mumbles things about a doorway where the roses bloom and
    smile;
If she mentions that the robins will be nesting after while;
If she sighs a little, sings a little, acts a little coy,
And your bosom starts to swelling with a new and foolish
    joy,
And the shivers start to coming up your spinal column—boy,
Count a hundred!

If her cheeks begin to color and her lips begin to look
Like an angel's that you saw once in a childhood story book;
If in some unguarded moment, seemingly, a lock of hair
Flutters over on your shoulder—and she lets it linger there;
If you look, and in her eyes you see a light superb, divine—
Like a salesman's eyes are wearing when you sign the dotted
     line,
Only deeper and demurer—brother, take a tip of mine:
Count a hundred!

—*Larry Flint.*

29

ENCOURAGEMENTS TO A LOVER

Why so pale and wan, fond lover?
     Prythee, why so pale?
Will, if looking well can't move her,
     Looking ill prevail?
     Prythee, why so pale?

Why so dull and mute, young sinner?
     Prythee, why so mute?
Will, when speaking well can't win her,
     Saying nothing do't?
     Prythee, why so mute?

Quit, quit, for shame! this will not move,
     This cannot take her;
If of herself she will not love,
     Nothing can make her:
     The Devil take her!

—*Sir J. Suckling.*

30

A TAKING GIRL

She took my hand in sheltered nooks,
She took my candy and my books,
She took that lustrous wrap of fur,
She took those gloves I bought for her.
She took my words of love and care,
She took my flowers, rich and rare,
She took my time for quite awhile,
She took my kisses, maid so shy—
She took, I must confess, my eye,
She took whatever I would buy.
And then she took another guy.

                    —*Anonymous.*

31

BALLADE OF FORGOTTEN LOVES

Some poets sing of sweethearts dead,
  Some sing of true loves far away;
Some sing of those that others wed,
  And some of idols turned to clay.
  I sing a pensive roundelay
To sweethearts of a doubtful lot,
  The passions vanished in a day—
The little loves that I've forgot.

For, as the happy years have sped,
  And golden dreams have changed to gray,
How oft the flame of love was fed
  By glance, or smile, from Maud or May,
  When wayward Cupid was at play;

Mere fancies, formed of who knows what,
 But still my debt I ne'er can pay—
The little loves that I've forgot.

O joyous hours forever fled!
 O sudden hopes that would not stay!
Held only by the slender thread
 Of memory that's all astray.
 Their very names I cannot say.
Time's will is done, I know them not;
 But blessings on them all, I pray—
The little loves that I've forgot.

L'envoi

Sweetheart, why foolish fears betray?
 Ours is the one true lovers' knot;
Note well the burden of my lay—
 The little loves that I've forgot.
    —Arthur Grissom.

32

OLD STUFF

If I go to see the play,
 Of the story I am certain;
Promptly it gets under way
 With the lifting of the curtain.
Builded all that's said and done
 On the ancient recipe—
'Tis the same old Two and One:
 A and B in love with C.

If I read the latest book,
 There's the mossy situation;

One may confidently look
　For the trite triangulation.
Old as time, but ever new,
　Seemingly, this tale of Three—
Same old yarn of One and Two:
　A and C in love with B.

If I cast my eyes around,
　Far and near and middle distance,
Still the formula is found
　In our everyday existence.
Everywhere I look I see—
　Fact or fiction, life or play—
Still the little game of Three:
　B and C in love with A.

While the ancient law fulfills,
　Myriad moons shall wane and wax.
Jack must have his pair of Jills,
　Jill must have her pair of Jacks.
　　　　　—Bert Leston Taylor.

33

THE LAY OF THE LOVER'S FRIEND

Air—"The days we went a-gipsying."

I would all womankind were dead,
　Or banished o'er the sea;
For they have been a bitter plague
　These last six weeks to me:
It is not that I'm touched myself,
　For that I do not fear;

No female face hath shown me grace
  For many a bygone year.
    But 'tis the most infernal bore,
      Of all the bores I know,
    To have a friend who's lost his heart
      A short time ago.

Whene'er we steam it to Blackwall,
  Or down to Greenwich run,
To quaff the pleasant cider cup,
  And feed on fish and fun;
Or climb the slopes of Richmond Hill,
  To catch a breath of air:
Then, for my sins, he straight begins
  To rave about his fair.
    Oh, 'tis the most tremendous bore,
      Of all the bores I know,
    To have a friend who's lost his heart
      A short time ago.

In vain you pour into his ear
  Your own confiding grief;
In vain you claim his sympathy,
  In vain you ask relief;
In vain you try to rouse him by
  Joke, repartee, or quiz;
His sole reply's a burning sigh,
  And "What a mind it is!"
    O Lord! it is the greatest bore,
      Of all the bores I know,
    To have a friend who's lost his heart
      A short time ago.

I've heard her thoroughly described
  A hundred times, I'm sure;
And all the while I've tried to smile,
  And patiently endure;
He waxes strong upon his pangs,
  And potters o'er his grog;
And still I say, in a playful way—
  "Why you're a lucky dog!"
    But oh! it is the heaviest bore,
      Of all the bores I know,
    To have a friend who's lost his heart
      A short time ago.

I really wish he'd do like me
  When I was young and strong;
I formed a passion every week,
  But never kept it long.
But he has not the sportive mood
  That always rescued me,
And so I would all women could
  Be banished o'er the sea.
    For 'tis the most egregious bore,
      Of all the bores I know
    To have a friend who's lost his heart
      A short time ago.
              —*William E. Aytoun.*

34

DEFENDANT'S SONG

When first my old, old love I knew
  My bosom swelled with joy;
My riches at her feet I threw—
  I was a lovesick boy!

No terms seemed extravagant
   Upon her to employ—
I used to mope, and sigh, and pant,
   Just like a lovesick boy!

But joy incessant palls the sense:
   And love, unchanged, will cloy,
And she became a bore intense
   Unto her lovesick boy!
With fitful glimmer burnt my flame
   And I grew cold and coy,
At last, one morning, I became
   Another's lovesick boy.
                —*W. S. Gilbert.*

35

BALLADE OF UNFORTUNATE MAMMALS

Love is sharper than stones or sticks;
   Lone as the sea, and a deeper blue;
Loud in the night as a clock that ticks;
   Longer lived than the Wandering Jew.
   Show me a love that was done and through,
Tell me a kiss escaped its debt!
   Son, to your death you'll pay your due—
Women and elephants never forget.

Ever a man, alas, would mix,
   Ever a man, heigh-ho, must woo;
So he's left in the world-old fix,
   Thus is furthered the sale of rue.
   Son, your chances are thin and few—
Won't you ponder before you're set?

Shoot if you must, but hold in view
Women and elephants never forget.

Down from Caesar past Joynson-Hicks
 Echoes the warning, ever new;
Though they're trained to amusing ticks,
 Gentler, they, than the pigeon's coo,
 Careful, son, of the cursed two—
Either one is a dangerous pet;
 Natural history proves it true—
Women and elephants never forget.

L'envoi

Prince, a precept I'd leave for you,
Coined in Eden, existing yet;
 Skirt the parlor and shun the zoo—
Women and elephants never forget.

—Dorothy Parker.

36

JOHN EVERELDOWN

"Where are you going to-night, to-night,—
 Where are you going, John Evereldown?
There's never the sign of a star in sight,
 Nor a lamp that's nearer than Tilbury Town.
Why do you stare as a dead man might?
Where are you pointing away from the light?
And where are you going to-night, to-night,—
 Where are you going, John Evereldown?"

"Right through the forest, where none can see,
 There's where I'm going, to Tilbury Town.
The men are asleep,—or awake, may be,—

But the women are calling John Evereldown.
Ever and ever they call for me,
And while they call can a man be free?
So right through the forest, where none can see,
    There's where I'm going, to Tilbury Town."

"But why are you going so late, so late,—
    Why are you going, John Evereldown?
Though the road be smooth and the way be straight,
    There are two long leagues to Tilbury Town.
Come in by the fire, old man, and wait!
Why do you chatter out there by the gate?
And why are you going so late, so late,—
    Why are you going, John Evereldown?"

"I follow the women wherever they call,—
    That's why I'm going to Tilbury Town.
God knows if I pray to be done with it all,
    But God is no friend to John Evereldown.
So the clouds may come and the rain may fall,
The shadows may creep and the dead men crawl,—
But I follow the women wherever they call,
    And that's why I'm going to Tilbury Town."
                    —*Edwin Arlington Robinson.*

37

THE BETROTHAL

Oh, come, my lad, or go, my lad,
And love me if you like.
I shall not hear the door shut
Nor the knocker strike.

Oh, bring me gifts or beg me gifts,
And wed me if you will.
I'd make a man a good wife,
Sensible and still.

And why should I be cold, my lad,
And why should you repine,
Because I love a dark head
That never will be mine?

I might as well be easing you
As lie alone in bed
And waste the night in wanting
A cruel dark head.

You might as well be calling yours
What never will be his,
And one of us be happy.
There's few enough as is.
                    —*Edna St. Vincent Millay.*

38

FINALLY

When you are tired of virtue
And I am tired of sin,
And nothing's left to hurt you,
And nothing's left to win,
Perhaps, O greatly daring,
Your eyes will question mine—
But shall I then be caring
For roses or for wine?
                    —*Vincent Starrett.*

II

THE STAG MURMURS
TO HIS MATE

Singing is sweet; but be sure of this—
Lips only sing when they cannot kiss.

—*James Thomson*

39

THE GOOD MORROW

I wonder, by my troth, what thou and I
  Did till we loved! Were we not weaned till then,
But sucked on country pleasures childishly?
  Or snorted we in the Seven Sleepers' den?
'Twas so; but thus all pleasures fancies be.
If ever any beauty I did see,
Which I desired and got,—'twas but a dream of thee.

.   .   .

—John Donne.

40

TO ANTHEA WHO MAY COMMAND HIM
ANY THING

Bid me to live, and I will live
  Thy Protestant to be:
Or bid me love, and I will give
  A loving heart to thee.

A heart as soft, a heart as kind,
  A heart as sound and free
As in the whole world thou canst find,
  That heart I'll give to thee.

Bid that heart stay, and it will stay,
  To honor thy decree:
Or bid it languish quite away,
  And 't shall do so for thee.

Bid me to weep, and I will weep
  While I have eyes to see:
And having none, yet I will keep
  A heart to weep for thee.

Bid me despair, and I'll despair,
  Under that cypress tree:
Or bid me die, and I will dare
  E'en Death, to die for thee.

Thou art my life, my love, my heart,
  The very eyes of me,
And hast command of every part,
  To live and die for thee.
        —*Robert Herrick.*

41

GO, LOVELY ROSE

Go, lovely Rose!
Tell her, that wastes her time and me,
  That now she knows,
When I resemble her to thee,
How sweet and fair she seems to be.

Tell her that's young
And shuns to have her graces spied,
  That hadst thou sprung
In deserts, where no men abide,
Thou must have uncommended died.

Small is the worth
Of beauty from the light retired:
  Bid her come forth,
Suffer herself to be desired,
And not blush so to be admired.

  Then die! that she
The common fate of all things rare
  May read in thee:
How small a part of time they share
They are so wondrous sweet and fair!
                    —*E. Waller.*

42

SONNETS

I

When, in disgrace with fortune and men's eyes,
I all alone beweep my outcast state,
And trouble deaf heaven with my bootless cries,
And look upon myself, and curse my fate,
Wishing me like to one more rich in hope,
Featur'd like him, like him with friends possess'd,
Desiring this man's art, and that man's scope,
With what I most enjoy contented least;
Yet in these thoughts myself almost despising,
Haply I think on thee,—and then my state,
Like to the lark at break of day arising
From sullen earth, sings hymns at heaven's gate;
  For thy sweet love remember'd such wealth brings
  That then I scorn to change my state with kings.

II

Who will believe my verse in time to come,
If it were fill'd with your most high deserts?
Though yet, heaven knows, it is but as a tomb
Which hides your life and shows not half your parts.
If I could write the beauty of your eyes
And in fresh numbers number all your graces,
The age to come would say, "This poet lies;
Such heavenly touches ne'er touch'd earthly faces."
So should my papers, yellow'd with their age,
Be scorn'd, like old men of less truth than tongue,
And your true rights be term'd a poet's rage
And stretched metre of an antique song:
    But were some child of yours alive that time,
    You should live twice,—in it and in my rime.

.   .   .

III

Since brass, nor stone, nor earth, nor boundless sea,
But sad mortality o'er sways their power,
How with this rage shall beauty hold a plea,
Whose action is no stronger than a flower?
O! how shall summer's honey breath hold out
Against the wrackful siege of battering days,
When rocks impregnable are not so stout,
Nor gates of steel so strong, but Time decays?
O fearful meditation! where, alack,
Shall Time's best jewel from Time's chest lie hid?
Or what strong hand can hold his swift foot back?
Or who his spoil of beauty can forbid?
    O! none, unless, this miracle have might,
    That in black ink my love may still shine bright.

.   .   .

IV

Then hate me when thou wilt; if ever, now;
Now, while the world is bent my deeds to cross,
Join with the spite of fortune, make me bow,
And do not drop in for an after-loss:
Ah! do not, when my heart hath 'scaped this sorrow,
Come in the rearward of a conquered woe;
Give not a windy night a rainy morrow,
To linger out a purposed overthrow.
If thou wilt leave me, do not leave me last,
When other petty griefs have done their spite,
But in the onset come; so shall I taste
At first the very worst of fortune's might;
   And other strains of woe, which now seem woe,
   Compared with loss of thee will not seem so.

                      —Shakespeare.

43

A VALEDICTION FORBIDDING MOURNING

As virtuous men pass mildly away,
And whisper to their souls to go:
Whilst some of their sad friends do say,
The breath goes now—and some say, no;

So let us melt, and make no noise,
No tear-floods, nor sigh-tempests move;
'Twere profanation of our joys
To tell the laity our love.

Moving of th' earth brings harms and fears,
Men reckon what it did, and meant;

But trepidation of the spheres,
Though greater far, is innocent.

Dull, sublunary lovers' love—
Whose soul is sense—cannot admit
Absence, because it doth remove
Those things which alimented it.

But we're by love so much refined,
That ourselves know not what it is;
Inter-assurèd of the mind,
Careless eyes, lips, and hands to miss.

Our two souls, therefore, (which are one)
Though I must go, endure not yet
A breach, but an expansion,
Like gold to airy thinness beat.

If they be two, they are two so
As stiff thin compasses are two;
Thy soul, the fix'd foot, makes no show
To move, but doth, if th' other do.

And though it in the centre sit,
Yet when the other far doth roam,
It leans, and hearkens after it,
And grows erect as that comes home.

Such wilt thou be to me, who must
Like th' other foot, obliquely run;
Thy firmness makes my circles just,
And makes me end where I begun.

                              —*John Donne.*

44

HEAVEN'S STARS

The night has a thousand eyes,
  My Sweetheart, two—
If ever the light of the stars should fail
  I know what God would do.
              —*Wightman F. Melton.*

45

ROMANCE

I will make you brooches and toys for your delight
Of bird-song at morning and star-shine at night.
I will make a palace fit for you and me,
Of green days in forests and blue days at sea.

I will make my kitchen, and you shall keep your room,
Where white flows the river and bright blows the broom,
And you shall wash your linen and keep your body white
In rainfall at morning and dewfall at night.

And this shall be for music when no one else is near,
The fine song for singing, the rare song to hear!
That only I remember, that only you admire,
Of the broad road that stretches and the roadside fire.
              —*Robert Louis Stevenson.*

46

OR EVER THE KNIGHTLY YEARS WERE GONE

Or ever the knightly years were gone
  With the old world to the grave,
I was a King in Babylon
  And you were a Christian Slave.

I saw, I took, I cast you by,
  I bent and broke your pride.
You loved me well, or I heard them lie,
  But your longing was denied.
Surely I knew that by and by
  You cursed your gods and died.

And a myriad suns have set and shone
  Since then upon the grave
Decreed by the King of Babylon
  To her that had been his Slave.

The pride I trampled is now my scathe,
  For it tramples me again.
The old resentment lasts like death,
  For you love, yet you refrain.
I break my heart on your hard unfaith,
  And I break my heart in vain.

Yet not for an hour do I wish undone
  The deed beyond the grave,
When I was a King in Babylon
  And you were a Virgin Slave.
                    —*William Ernest Henley.*

47

LOVE'S PHILOSOPHY

The fountains mingle with the river
  And the rivers with the Ocean,
The winds of Heaven mix for ever
  With a sweet emotion;

Nothing in the world is single;
   All things by a law divine
In one spirit meet and mingle.
   Why not I with thine?—

See the mountains kiss high Heaven
   And the waves clasp one another;
No sister-flower would be forgiven
   If it disdained its brother;
And the sunlight clasps the earth
   And the moonbeams kiss the sea:
What is all this sweet work worth
   If thou kiss not me?
            —*Percy Bysshe Shelley.*

48

AMORETTI

.   .   .

One day I wrote her name upon the strand,
But came the waves and washed it away:
Again I wrote it with a second hand,
But came the tide and made my pains his prey.
"Vain man," said she, "that dost in vain essay
A mortal thing so to immortalize;
For I myself shall like to this decay,
And eke my name be wiped out likewise."
"Not so," quoth I; "let baser things devise
To die in dust, but you shall live by fame;
My verse your virtues rare shall eternize,
And in the heavens write your glorious name:

Where, whenas Death shall all the world subdue,
Our love shall live, and later life renew."

. . .

—*Edmund Spenser.*

49

INDIA'S LOVE LYRICS

As arranged by *Laurence Hope*

"To the Unattainable"

Oh, that my blood were water, thou athirst,
And thou and I in some far Desert land,
How would I shed it gladly, if but first
It touched thy lips, before it reached the sand. . . .

. . .

But thou; Alas, what can I do for thee?
By Fate, and thine own beauty, set above
The need of all or any aid from me,
Too high for service, as too far for love.

Thoughts: Mahomed Akram

If some day this body of mine were burned
(It found no favour alas! with you)
And the ashes scattered abroad, unurned,
Would Love die also, would Thought die too?
  But who can answer, or who can trust,
  No dreams would harry the windblown dust?

Were I laid away in the furrows deep
Secure from jackal and passing plough,
Would your eyes not follow me still through sleep
Torment me then as they torture now?
   Would you ever have loved me, Golden Eyes,
   Had I done aught better or otherwise?

Was I overspeechful, or did you yearn
When I sat silent, for songs or speech?
Oh, Beloved, I had been so apt to learn,
So apt, had you only cared to teach.
   But time for silence and song is done,
   You wanted nothing, my Golden Sun!

What should you want of a waning star?
That drifts in its lonely orbit far
Away from your soft, effulgent light
In outer planes of Eternal night?

The Teak Forest

Whether I loved you who shall say?
Whether I drifted down your way
In the endless River of Chance and Change,
And you woke the strange
Unknown longings that have no names,
But burn us all in their hidden flames,
   Who shall say?

Life is a strange and wayward thing:
We heard the bells of the Temples ring,
The married children, in passing, sing.
The month of marriage, the month of spring,
Was full of the breath of sunburnt flowers

That bloom in a fiercer light than ours,
And, under a sky more fiercely blue,
    I came to you!

You told me tales of your vivid life
Where death was cruel and danger rife—
Of deep dark forests, of poisoned trees,
Of pains and passions that scorch and freeze,
Of southern noontides and eastern nights,
Where love grew frantic with strange delights,
While men were slaying and maidens danced,
Till I, who listened, lay still, entranced.
Then, swift as a swallow heading south,
    I kissed your mouth!

One night when the plains were bathed in blood
From sunset light in a crimson flood,
We wandered under the young teak trees
Whose branches whined in the light night breeze;
You led me down to the water's brink,
"The Spring where the Panthers come to drink
At night; there is always water here
Be the season never so parched and sere."
Have we souls of beasts in the forms of men?
I fain would have tasted your life-blood then.

The night fell swiftly; this sudden land
Can never lend us a twilight strand
'Twixt the daylight shore and the ocean night,
But takes—as it gives—at once, the light.
We laid us down on the steep hillside,
While far below us wild peacocks cried,
And we sometimes heard, in the sunburnt grass,
The stealthy steps of the Jungle pass.

We listened; knew not whether they went
On love or hunger the more intent.
And under your kisses I hardly knew
Whether I loved or hated you.

But your words were flame and your kisses fire,
And who shall resist a strong desire?
Not I, whose life is a broken boat
On a sea of passions, adrift, afloat.
And, whether I came in love or hate,
That I came to you was written by Fate
In every hue of the blood-red sky,
In every tone of the peacocks' cry.

While every gust of the Jungle night
Was fanning the flame you had set alight.
For these things have power to stir the blood
And compel us all to their own chance mood.
And to love or not we are no more free
Than a ripple to rise and leave the sea.

We are ever and always slaves of these,
Of the suns that scorch and the winds that freeze,
Of the faint sweet scents of the sultry air,
Of the half heard howl from the far off lair.
These chance things master us ever. Compel
To the heights of Heaven, the depths of Hell.

Whether I love you? You do not ask,
Nor waste yourself on the thankless task.
I give your kisses at least return,
What matter whether they freeze or burn.
I feel the strength of your fervent arms,
What matter whether it heals or harms.

You are wise; you take what the Gods have sent.
You ask no question, but rest content
So I am with you to take your kiss,
And perhaps I value you more for this.
For this is Wisdom; to love, to live,
To take what Fate, or the Gods, may give,
To ask no question, to make no prayer,
To kiss the lips and caress the hair,
Speed passion's ebb as you greet its flow,—
To have,—to hold,—and,—in time,—let go!

And this is our Wisdom: we rest together
On the great lone hills in the storm-filled weather,
And watch the skies as they pale and burn,
The golden stars in their orbits turn,
While Love is with us, and Time and Peace,
And life has nothing to give but these.
But, whether you love me, who shall say,
Or whether you, drifting down my way
In the great sad River of Chance and Change,
With your looks so weary and words so strange,
Lit my soul from some hidden flame
To a passionate longing without a name,
    Who shall say?
Not I, who am but a broken boat,
Content for awhile to drift afloat
In the little noontide of love's delights
    Between two Nights.

But half a love is treason, that no Lover can forgive,
I had loved you for a season, I had no more to give.
You saw my passion faltered, for I could but let you see,
And it was not I that altered, but Fate that altered me.

.   .   .

He died, he died, I speak the truth,
   Though light love leaves his memory dim.
He was the Lover of my Youth
   And all my youth went down with him.

50

NON SUM QUALIS ERAM BONAE
SUB REGNO CYNARAE

Last Night, ah, yesternight, betwixt her lips and mine
There fell they shadow, Cynara! thy breath was shed
Upon my soul between the kisses and the wine;
And I was desolate and sick of an old passion,
   Yea, I was desolate and bowed my head:
I have been faithful to thee, Cynara! in my fashion.

All night upon mine heart I felt her warm heart beat,
Night-long within mine arms in love and sleep she lay;
Surely the kisses of her bought red mouth were sweet;
But I was desolate and sick of an old passion,
   When I awoke and found the dawn was gray:
I have been faithful to thee, Cynara! in my fashion.

I have forgot much, Cynara! gone with the wind,
Flung roses, roses riotously with the throng,
Dancing, to put thy pale, lost lilies out of mind;
But I was desolate and sick of an old passion,
   Yea, all the time, because the dance was long:
I have been faithful to thee, Cynara! in my fashion.

I cried for madder music and for stronger wine,
But when the feast is finished and the lamps expire,
Then falls thy shadow, Cynara! the night is thine;
And I am desolate and sick of an old passion,
   Yea, hungry for the lips of my desire:
I have been faithful to thee, Cynara! in my fashion.
                  —Ernest Dowson.

51

TO HIS MISTRESS

There comes an end to summer,
   To spring showers and hoar rime;
His mumming to each mummer
   Has somewhere end in time,
And since life ends and laughter,
   And leaves fall and tears dry,
Who shall call love immortal,
   When all that is must die?

Nay, sweet, let's leave unspoken
   The vows the fates gainsay,
For all vows made are broken,
   We love but while we may.
Let's kiss when kissing pleases,
   And part when kisses pall,
Perchance, this time to-morrow,
   We shall not love at all.

You ask my love completest,
   As strong next year as now,
The devil take you, sweetest,
   Ere I make aught such vow.

Life is a masque that changes,
  A fig for constancy!
No love at all were better,
  Than love which is not free.
—Ernest Dowson.

52

FREE LOVE

My love must be as free
  As is the eagle's wing,
Hovering o'er land and sea
  And everything.

I must not dim my eye
  In thy saloon,
I must not leave my sky
  And nightly moon.

Be not the fowler's net
  Which stays my flight,
And craftily is set
  T' allure the sight.

But be the favoring gale
  That bears me on,
And still doth fill my sail
  When thou art gone.

I cannot leave my sky
  For thy caprice,
True love would soar as high
  As heaven is.

The eagle would not brook
Her mate thus won,
Who trained his eye to look
Beneath the sun.
—*Henry David Thoreau.*

53

⚔ SINCE THERE'S NO HELP

Since there's no help, come, let us kiss and part,—
Nay I have done, you get no more of me;
And I am glad, yea glad with all my heart,
That thus so cleanly I myself can free;
Shake hands for ever, cancel all our vows,
And when we meet at any time again,
Be it not seen in either of our brows
That we one jot of former love retain.
Now at the last gasp of Love's latest breath,
When his pulse failing, Passion speechless lies,
When Faith is kneeling by his bed of death,
And Innocence is closing up his eyes,—
　Now if thou would'st, when all have given him over,
　From death to life thou might'st him yet recover!
—*Michael Drayton.*

54

THE NIGHT HAS A THOUSAND EYES

The night has a thousand eyes,
And the day but one;
Yet the light of the bright world dies
With the dying sun.

The mind has a thousand eyes,
   And the heart but one;
Yet the light of a whole life dies
   When love is done.
     —*Francis William Bourdillon.*

55

IF I HAVE MADE, MY LADY

if i have made, my lady, intricate
imperfect various things chiefly which wrong
your eyes (frailer than most deep dreams are frail)
songs less firm than your body's whitest song
upon my mind—if i have failed to snare
the glance too shy—if through my singing slips
the very skillful strangeness of your smile
the keen primeval silence of your hair

—let the world say "his most wise music stole
nothing from death"—
             you only will create
(who are so perfectly alive) my shame:
   lady through whose profound and fragile lips
   the sweet small clumsy feet of April came

into the ragged meadow of my soul.
           —*e. e. cummings.*

56

WHEN TROUT SWIM DOWN GREAT ORMOND STREET

When trout swim down Great Ormond Street.
And sea-gulls cry above them lightly,

And hawthorns heave cold flagstones up
To blossom whitely,

Against old walls of houses there,
Gustily shaking out in moonlight
Their country sweetness on sweet air;
And in the sunlight,

By the green margin of that water,
Children dip white feet and shout,
Casting nets in the braided water
To catch the trout:

Then I shall hold my breath and die,
Swearing I never loved you; no,
'You were not lovely!' I shall cry,
'I never loved you so.'

—*Conrad Aiken.*

57

LOVER TO LOVER

Leave me a while, for you have been too long
A nearness that is perilous and sweet:
Loose me a little from the tightening thong
That binds my spirit, eyes and hands and feet.
For there are old communions I would hold,
To mind my heart what field and sky may be:
Earth bears her fruit . . . November has a gold . . .
And stars are still high points in constancy.
Loose me a little, now . . . I have a need
Of standing in an open, windy place,
Of saying names again, of giving heed

To these companions of man's lonely race . . .
Loose me to these, between one dusk and dawn;—
I shall have need of them, when you are gone.

                              —*David Morton.*

58

ASK ME TONIGHT

Ask me tonight why love is strange—
    For I am drunk and full of reasons—
Why maids our lives must disarrange,
    And loves must perish with the seasons;
Why life is all that men have said,
    And much that none has dared to write.
If you would have this riddle read,
    Ask me tonight!

Ask me tonight—for I am drunk—
    Why love is fire and fire is ashes;
Why he is happier than a monk,
    Who says his prayers to pensive lashes.
Tomorrow I shall play my part,
    Forgetting that your eyes are bright.
If you would know my secret heart,
    Ask me tonight.

                              —*Vincent Starrett.*

59

GHOST

I'm comin' back and haunt you, don't you fret.
    What if I get as far as Hell away?

They's things of me that just can't help but stay—
Whether I want or not, you can't forget.

Just when you think you got me wiped out clear,
    Some bird that's singin'—moonlight on a hill—
    Some lovely thing'll hurt like it would kill,
And you'll hear somethin' whisperin', "He's here!"

And when somebody holds you closte, like this,
    And you start in to feel your pulses race,
    The face that's pressin' yours'll be my face;
My lips'll be the ones your lips'll kiss.

Don't cry . . . Which do you think it'll hurt most?—
Oh, God! You think I *want* to be a ghost? . . .

                              —*John V. A. Weaver.*

III

WEDLOCK'S WOE AND WEAL

What? Rise again with *all* one's bones,
    Quoth Giles, I hope you fib.
I trusted when I went to Heaven,
    To go without my rib.

                    —*Samuel Taylor Coleridge.*

60

ON BEING ADVISED TO MARRY

Sir, you are prudent, good and wise,
    I own and thank you from my heart;
And much approve what you advise,
    But let me think before I start.

For folks well able to discern,
    Who know what 'tis to take a wife,
Say 'tis a case of such concern
    A man should think on 't—all his life.

61

WEDLOCK

A scholar newly entered marriage life,
Following his studies, did offend his wife;
Because when she his company expected
By bookish business she was still neglected.
Coming into his study, Lord (quoth she),
Can papers cause you love them more than me?
I would I were transformed into a book,
That your affection might upon me look;
But in my wish withal it be decreed
I would be such a book you love to read.
Husband (quoth she), which book's form should
    I take?
Marry (said he), 'twere best an almanake.
The reason wherefore I do wish thee so
Is, every year we have a new, you know.

                  —Samuel Rowland.

62

ON A SCOLD

Here lies a woman, no man can deny it,
Who rests in peace, although she lived unquiet,
Her husband prays you, if by her grave you walk
You gently tread, for if she wake, she'll talk.

—(*Sixteenth Century Epigram.*)

63

THE JOYS OF MARRIAGE

How uneasy is his life,
Who is troubled with a wife!
Be she ne'er so fair or comely,
Be she ne'er so foul or homely,
Be she ne'er so young and toward,
Be she ne'er so old and froward.
Be she kind, with arms enfolding,
Be she cross, and always scolding,
Be she blithe or melancholy,
Have she wit, or have she folly,
Be she wary, be she squandering,
Be she staid, or be she wandering,
Be she constant, be she fickle,
Be she fire, or be she ickle;
Be she pious or ungodly,
Be she chaste, or what sounds oddly:
Lastly, be she good or evil,
Be she saint, or be she devil,—
Yet, uneasy is his life
Who is married to a wife.

—*Charles Cotton.*

64

PARADISE

A Hindoo Legend

A Hindoo died—a happy thing to do
When twenty years united to a shrew.
Released, he hopefully for entrance cries
Before the gates of Brahma's Paradise.
"Has been through Purgatory?" Brahma said.
"I have been married," and he hung his head.
"Come in, come in, and welcome, too my son!
Marriage and Purgatory are as one."
In bliss extreme he entered heaven's door,
And knew the peace he ne'er had known before.

He scarce had entered in the Garden fair,
Another Hindoo asked admission there.
The self-same question Brahma asked again:
"Has been through Purgatory?" "No; what then?"
"Thou canst not enter!" did the god reply.
"He that went in was no more there than I."
"Yes, that is true, but he has married been,
And so on earth has suffered for all sin."
"Married? 'Tis well; for I've been married twice!"
"Begone! We'll have no fools in Paradise!"

—*George Birdseye.*

65

THE WOMAN WHO UNDERSTANDS

*SOMEWHERE she waits to make you win, your soul
in her firm, white hands—
Somewhere the gods have made for you, the Woman
Who Understands!*

As the tide went out she found him
   Lashed to a spar of Despair,
The wreck of his Ship around him—
   The wreck of his Dreams in the air;
Found him and loved him and gathered
   The soul of him close to her heart—
The soul that had sailed an uncharted sea,
The soul that had sought to win and be free—
   The soul of which *she* was part!
     And there in the dusk she cried to the man,
     "Win your battle—you can, you can!"

Broken by Fate, unrelenting,
   Scarred by the lashings of Chance;
Bitter his heart—unrepenting—
   Hardened by Circumstance;
Shadowed by Failure ever,
   Cursing, he would have died,
But the touch of her hand, her strong warm hand,
And her love of his soul, took full command,
   Just at the turn of the tide!
     Standing beside him, filled with trust,
     "Win!" she whispered, "you must, you must!"

Helping and loving and guiding,
   Urging when that were best,
Holding her fears in hiding
   Deep in her quiet breast;
This is the woman who kept him
   True to his standards lost,
When, tossed in the storm and stress of strife,
He thought himself through with the game of life
   And ready to pay the cost.
     Watching and guarding, whispering still,
     "Win you can—and you will, you will!"

This is the story of ages,
　　This is the Woman's way;
Wiser than seers or sages,
　　Lifting us day by day;
Facing all things with a courage
　　Nothing can daunt or dim,
Treading Life's path, wherever it leads—
Lined with flowers or choked with weeds,
　　But ever with him—with him!
　　　　Guide—comrade—golden spur—
　　　　The men who win are helped by *her!*

*Somewhere she waits, strong in belief, your soul in her
　　firm, white hands:
Thank well the gods, when she comes to you—the
　　Woman Who Understands!*
　　　　　　　　　　—*Everard Jack Appleton.*

66

MENTAL INFLATION

How often does it happen that we love to make a show
Of wisdom, though the theme is one of which we little
　　know.
The other night young Mr. B., in most painstaking style,
Explained financial problems to his wife for quite a while.
"I see," he said in closing, "you're impressed decidedly
By my clear explanation about banks and currency."
"Oh yeah?" said wife, "and think how you, mid tribulations
　　many,
Know so much about money, dear, without possessing any!"
　　　　　　　　　　—*Fred Clifford.*

67

MY WIFE

Trusty, dusky, vivid, true,
With eyes of gold and bramble-dew,
Steel-true, and blade-straight,
The great Artificer
Made my mate.

Honour, anger, valour, fire;
A love that life could never tire,
Death quench or evil stir,
The mighty Master
Gave to her.

Teacher, tender comrade, wife,
A fellow-farer true through life,
Heart-whole and soul-free
The august Father
Gave to me.
—*Robert Louis Stevenson.*

68

FOR ANNIVERSARY MARRIAGE-DAYS

Lord, living, here are we
As fast united yet
As when our hands and hearts by Thee
Together first were knit,
And, in a thankful song,
Now sing we will Thy praise,

For, that Thou dost as well prolong
  Our loving as our days.

Together we have now
  Begun another year;
But how much time Thou wilt allow
  Thou mak'st it not appear.
  We, therefore, do implore
  That live and love we may,
Still so, as if but one day more
  Together we should stay.

Let each of other's wealth
  Preserve a faithful care,
And of each other's joy and health,
  As if one soul we were.
  Such conscience let us make,
  Each other not to grieve,
As if we, daily, were to take
  Our everlasting-leave.

The frowardness that springs
  From our corrupted king,
Or from those troublous outward things,
  Which may distract the mind,
  Permit Thou not, O Lord,
  Our constant love to shake;
Or to disturb our true accord,
  Or make our hearts to ache.

But let these frailties prove
  Affection's exercize;
And that discretion teach our love
  Which wins the noblest prize.

So Time which wears away
And ruins all things else
Shall fix our love on Thee for aye
In whom perfection dwells.
                    —*George Wither.*

69

SUCCESS

They said he was a failure since
    He won nor eminence nor fame,
And no one but his friends were stirred
    At any mention of his name.

Ah, foolish ones, they could not gauge
    The measurement of his success—
He left his friends glad memories,
    And gave one woman happiness.
                    —*Charlotte Becker.*

70

POST-MORTEM

So you have gone, and here within this room
    Where we have loved each small thing speaks of
        you,
And this, that was a palace, is a tomb,
    And I have wept as you would wish me to.
Wearied and effortless, I lie alone,
    Certain of only this, since you have gone;
The law of love is like a hard, bright stone—
    And all your pretty words stay on and on;

I count the echoes unbelievingly,
   I shred my mind with hope and fear and pain,
While you walk on to other loves than me,
   And my desire will not touch you again.

   Your mouth was but a lie, your arms a snare . . .
   Why did you leave your slippers by the chair?
                           —*Jane Sayre.*

IV

THE STAG AND THE
SCARLET STAIN

No, no; for my virginity,
When I lose that, says Rose, I'll die:
Behind the elms, last night, cried Dick,
Rose, were you not extremely sick?

—Matthew Prior.

SISTERS OF THE CROSS OF SHAME

The Sisters of the Cross of Shame,
They smile along the night;
Their houses stand with shuttered souls
And painted eyes of light.

Their houses look with scarlet eyes
Upon a world of sin;
And every man cries, "Woe, alas!"
And every man goes in.

The sober Senate meets at noon,
To pass the Woman's law,
The churchmen vote to stem
The torrent with a straw.

The Sister of the Cross of Shame,
She smiles beneath her cloud,
(She does not laugh till ten o'clock
And then she laughs too loud.)

And still she hears the throb of feet
Upon the scarlet stair,
And still she dons the cloak of shame
That is not hers to wear.

The sons of saintly women come
To kiss the Cross of Shame;
Before them in another time,
Their worthy fathers came.

And no man tells his son the truth,
Lest he should speak of sin;
And every man cries, "Woe, alas!"
And every man goes in.

                        —*Dana Burnet.*

72

MARIA PERIPATETICA

Sad, painted flower, cast unwist
Into Life's lap; poor face that Fate
Has mocked at, drunk to, smitten, kissed,
Until I read the rune thereof
With more in it to love than hate,
With more to pity than to love—

What nights were thine! What morns were their's
Whose sleep was incense, vital, rare,
Burned into ashes unawares
Before thy desecrated shrine!—
Thy barren bosom freed their cares,
Because its milk was bitter wine.

Of all who loved and let thee go
Is there not one whose lips impressed
Their stamp upon thy memory so—
Or dark or fair, or black or white—
His eyes outsparkle all the rest,
The casual Antonies of a night?

Of all the mouths thy mouth hath drained,
Of all the breasts thy breasts have sought
And clung to, mad, desired, disdained,

In that long catalogue of dole
Is there not one who something taught,
His soul embracing thy lost soul?

That fair first lover on whose head
Thy maiden shame and passion place—
Living and loving, or purged and dead—
So rich a crown of memory
That to thine inmost heart his face
A sinning saint's seems—is it he?

Or is it some poor drunken fool,
Wiser than thou—God save the mark!—
In that salacious, brutal school
Where beasts, as thou and I are, sweat
Over the lesson of the Dark,
That thou recall'st with dear regret?

Perhaps some country lad who came
Fresh from his home to town and thee
Is closest, his the charmed name,
Who, with the parting tears fresh shed
With all his sweet virginity
Thy sacramental table spread.

My canker-eaten rose, what then?
My scape-goat of an out-worn code,
"All things," said Paul, "unto all men"—
So thou who with the setting sun
Farest nightly on the endless road,
To all men mistress, wife to none!

But mine tonight, though not to kiss!
I lay my head upon that breast
Whose scar our sister's safety is,

And, from our darkest misery,
To beg thy mercy is my quest,
Lest that we perish utterly.

Forgive our women's scornful glance,
Our poor, pale, pure maids decorous,
Virgins by purse and circumstance;
Forgive the tearing tusk and claw;
Forgive the law that made thee thus;—
Forgive the God who made the law!
                    —*Reginald Wright Kauffman.*

73

SEE-SAW

She was a harlot, and I was a thief:
But we loved each other beyond belief:
She lived in the garret, and I in the kitchen,
And love was all that we both were rich in.

When they sent her at last to the hospital,
Both day and night my tears did fall.
They fell so fast that, to dry their grief,
I borrowed my neighbor's handkerchief.

The world, which, as it is brutally taught,
Still judges the act in lieu of the thought,
Found my hand in my neighbor's pocket,
And clapped me, at once, under chain and locket.

When they asked me about it, I told them plain,
Love it was that had turned my brain:
How should I heed where my hand had been,
When my heart was dreaming of Celestine?

Twelve friends were so struck by my woful air,
That they sent me abroad for change of air:
And, to prove me the kindness of their intent,
They sent me at charge of the Government.

When I came back again,—whom, think you, I meet
But Celestine, here, in Regent Street?
In a carriage adorned with a coronet,
And a dress, all flounces, and lace, and jet:

For her carriage drew up to the bookseller's door,
Where they publish those nice little books for the poor:
I took off my hat: and my face she knew,
And gave me—a sermon by Mr. Belew.

But she gave me (God bless her!) along with the book,
Such a sweet sort of smile, such a heavenly look,
That, as long as I live, I shall never forget
Celestine, in her coach with the earl's coronet.

There's a game that men play at in great London-town:
Whereby some must go up, sir, and some must go down:
And, since the mud sticks to your coat if you fall,
Why, the strongest among us keep close to the wall.

But some day, soon or late, in my shoes I shall stand,
More exalted than any great duke in the land;
A clean shirt on my back, and a rose in my coat,
And a collar conferred by the Queen round my throat.

And I know that my Celestine will not forget
To be there, in her coach with my lord's coronet:
She will smile to me then, as she smiled to me now:
I shall nod to her gayly, and make her my bow;—

Before I rejoin all those famous old thieves
Whose deeds have immortalized Rome, sir, and Greece:
Whose names are inscribed upon History's leaves,
Like my own on the books of the City Police:—
Alexander, and Caesar, and other great robbers,
Who once tried to pocket the whole universe:
Not to speak of our own parliamentary jobbers,
With their hands, bless them all, in the popular purse!

—*Owen Meredith.*

74

THE RUINED MAID

"O 'Melia, my dear, this does everything crown!
Who could have supposed I should meet you in town?
And whence such fair garments, such prosperi-ty?"—
"O didn't you know I'd been ruined?" said she.

—"You left us in tatters, without shoes or socks,
Tired of digging potatoes, and spudding up docks;
And now you've gay bracelets and bright feathers
      three!"—
"Yes: that's how we dress when we're ruined," said she.

—"At home in the barton you said 'thee' and 'thou,'
And 'thik oon,' and 'Theas oon!' and 't'other'; but now
Your talking quite fits 'ee for high compa-ny!"—
"Some polish is gained with one's ruin," said she.

—"Your hands were like paws then, your face blue and
      bleak,
But now I'm bewitched by your delicate cheek,
And your little gloves fit as on any la-dy!"—
"We never do work when we're ruined," said she.

—"You used to call home-life a hag-ridden dream,
And you'd sigh, and you'd sock; but at present you seem
To know not of megrims or melanchol-ly!"
"True. There's an advantage in ruin," said she.

—"I wish I had feathers, a fine sweeping gown,
And a delicate face, and could strut about town!"—
"My dear—a raw country girl, such as you be,
Isn't equal to that. You ain't ruined," said she.

—*Thomas Hardy.*

V

THE CONVIVIAL STAG

If all be true that I do think,

There are five reasons we should drink:

Good wine—a friend—or being dry—

Or lest we should be by and by—

Or any other reason why.

—*Henry Aldrich.*

75

CAUTION

Saint Patrick was a gentleman,
Who through strategy and stealth,
Drove all the snakes from Ireland—
Here's a bumper to his health.
But not too many bumpers,
Lest we lose ourselves, and then
Forget the good Saint Patrick
And see the snakes again.

—Anonymous.

76

GOD LYAEUS

God Lyaeus, ever young,
Ever honoured, ever sung;
Stained with blood of lusty grapes,
In a thousand lusty shapes
Dance upon the Mazer's brim,
In the crimson liquor swim;
From thy plenteous hand divine
Let a river run with wine;
 God of Youth, let this day here
 Enter neither care nor fear.

—John Fletcher.

77

JOHN BARLEYCORN

There were three kings into the east,
Three kings both great and high;

And they hae sworn a solemn oath
  John Barleycorn should die.

They took a plough and plough'd him down,
  Put clods upon his head;
And they hae sworn a solemn oath
  John Barleycorn was dead.

But the cheerful spring came kindly on,
  And showers began to fall:
John Barleycorn got up again,
  And sore surprised them all.

The sultry suns of summer came,
  And he grew thick and strong;
His head weel arm'd wi' pointed spears,
  That no one should him wrong.

The sober autumn enter'd mild,
  When he grew wan and pale;
His bending joints and drooping head
  Show'd he began to fail.

His colour sicken'd more and more,
  He faded into age;
And then his enemies began
  To show their deadly rage.

They've ta'en a weapon, long and sharp,
  And cut him by the knee;
Then tied him fast upon a cart,
  Like a rogue for forgerie.

They laid him down upon his back,
   And cudgell'd him full sore;
They hung him up before the storm,
   And turn'd him o'er and o'er.

They fillèd up a darksome pit
   With water to the brim:
They heavèd in John Barleycorn,
   There let him sink or swim.

They laid him out upon the floor,
   To work him further woe:
And still, as signs of life appear'd,
   They toss'd him to and fro.

They wasted o'er a scorching flame
   The marrow of his bones;
But a miller used him worst of all—
   He crush'd him 'tween two stones.

And they hae ta'en his very heart's blood,
   And drank it round and round,
And still the more and more they drank,
   Their joy did more abound.

John Barleycorn was a hero bold,
   Of noble enterprise;
For if you do but taste his blood,
   'Twill make your courage rise.

'Twill make a man forget his woe;
   'Twill heighten all his joy:
'Twill make the widow's heart to sing,
   Though the tear were in her eye.

Then let us toast John Barleycorn,
Each man a glass in hand;
And may his great posterity
Ne'er fail in old Scotland!
—*Robert Burns.*

78

THE CURE FOR ALL CARE

No churchman am I for to rail and to write,
No statesman nor soldier to plot or to fight,
No sly man of business contriving a snare;
For a big-bellied bottle's the whole of my care.

The peer I don't envy, I give him his bow;
I scorn not the peasant, though ever so low;
But a club of good fellows, like those that are here,
And a bottle like this, are my glory and care.

The wife of my bosom, alas! she did die;
For sweet consolation to church I did fly;
I found that old Solomon proved it fair,
That a big-bellied bottle's a cure for all care.

I once was persuaded a venture to make:
A letter informed me that all was to wreck;
But the pursy old landlord just waddled up stairs,
With a glorious bottle that ended my cares.

Life's cares, they are comforts—a maxim laid down
By the bard, what d'ye call him, that wore the black
gown;

And, faith, I agree with th' old prig to a hair;
For a big-bellied bottle's a heaven of care.

ADDED IN A MASON LODGE

Then fill up a bumper, and make it o'erflow,
And honors masonic prepare for to throw;
May every true brother of th' compass and square
Have a big-bellied bottle when harassed with care!

—Robert Burns.

79

If ever I marry a wife,
  I'll marry a landlord's daughter,
And sit in the bar all day,
  And drink cold brandy and water.

—Charles Lamb.

80

DRINKING

The thirsty earth soaks up the rain,
And drinks and gapes for drink again;
The plants suck in the earth, and are
With constant drinking fresh and fair;
The sea itself (which one would think
Should have but little need of drink)
Drinks twice ten thousand rivers up,
So fill'd that they o'erflow the cup.
The busy Sun (and one would guess
By 's drunken fiery face no less)
Drinks up the sea, and when he's done,

The Moon and Stars drink up the Sun:
They drink and dance by their own light,
They drink and revel all the night:
Nothing in Nature's sober found,
But an eternal health goes round.
Fill up the bowl, then, fill it high,
Fill all the glasses there—for why
Should every creature drink but I?
Why, man of morals, tell me why?
                    —*Abraham Cowley.*

81

BALLAD OF GOOD DOCTRINE TO THOSE OF ILL LIFE

Peddle indulgences, as you may:
    Cog the dice for your cheating throws:
Try if counterfeit coin will pay,
    At risk of roasting at last, like those
    That deal in treason. Lie and glose,
Rob and ravish: what profits it?
    Who gets the purchase, do you suppose?
Taverns and wenches, every whit.

Rhyme, rail, wrestle and cymbals play:
    Flute and fool it in mummers' shows:
Along with the strolling players stray
    From town to city, without repose;
    Act mysteries, farces, imbroglios;
Win money at gleek or at lucky hit
    At the pins: like water, away it flows;
Taverns and wenches, every whit.

Turn from your evil courses I pray,
   That smell so foul in a decent nose:
Earn your bread in some honest way.
   If you have no letters, nor verse nor prose,
   Plough or groom horses, beat hemp or toze.
Enough shall you have if you think but fit:
   But cast not your wage to each wind that blows;
Taverns and wenches, every whit.

Envoy

Doublets, pourpoints and silken hose,
   Gowns and linen, woven or knit,
Ere your wede's worn, away it goes;
   Taverns and wenches, every whit.

               —*Francois Villon.*

82

ROSY WINE

My Mistress' frowns are hard to bear,
And yet I will not quite despair;
Nor think, because her lips I leave,
There's nothing for me but to grieve.
—The goblet's lip awaiteth mine:
My grief I quench in rosy wine.

Dame Fortune too has faithless gone:
But let her go! I will not moan.
Draw in your chair, old Friend! and see
What rating Fortune has from me.
Clink yet again your glass with mine,—
To Fortune's health, in rosy wine!

Pass, Fortune! pass, thou fickle jade!
One fortunately constant maid
Smiles on me yet; though loves depart,
Her presence gladdeneth my heart,
Thy tendrils cling, O loving Vine!
My griefs I quench in rosy wine.
                              —*W. J. Linton.*

83

I'M VERY FOND OF WATER

A New Temperance Song
(Adapted from the Platt Deutsch)

I'm very fond of water,
　　I drink it noon and night:
Not Rechab's son or daughter
　　Had therein more delight.

I breakfast on it daily;
　　And nectar it doth seem,
When once I've mixed it gaily
　　With sugar and with cream.
But I forgot to mention—
　　That in it first I see
Infused or in suspension,
　　Good Mocha or Bohea.

Chorus—
I'm very fond of water,
　　I drink it noon and night;
No mother's son or daughter
　　Hath therein more delight.

At luncheon, too, I drink it,
   And strength it seems to bring:
When really good, I think it
   A liquor for a king.
But I forgot to mention—
   'Tis best to be sincere—
I use an old invention
   That makes it into Beer.
      I'm very fond of water, etc.

I drink it, too, at dinner;
   I quaff it full and free,
And find, as I'm a sinner,
   It does not disagree,
But I forgot to mention—
   As thus I drink and dine,
To obviate distension,
   I join some Sherry wine.
      I'm very fond of water, etc.

And then when dinner's over,
   And business far away,
I feel myself in clover,
   And sip my *eau sucrée.*
But I forgot to mention—
   To give the glass a smack,
I add, with due attention,
   Glenlivet or Cognac.
      I'm very fond of water, etc.

At last when evening closes,
   With something nice to eat,
The best of sleeping doses
   In water still I meet.

But I forgot to mention—
  I think it not a sin
To cheer the day's declension,
  By pouring in some Gin.
I'm very fond of water:
  It ever must delight
Each mother's son or daughter—
  When qualified aright.
                    —*Lord Neaves.*

84

R-E-M-O-R-S-E

This selection originally appeared in the comic opera, *The Sultan of Sulu,* and has been widely copied, with many variations. The authentic version printed here was personally typed for us by the author.

The cocktail is a pleasant drink;
It's mild and harmless—I don't think.
When you've had one, you call for two,
And then you don't care what you do.
Last night I hoisted twenty-three
Of those arrangements into me.
My wealth increased, I swelled with pride,
I was pickled, primed, and ossified;
But R-E-M-O-R-S-E!
The water wagon is the place for me.
Last night at twelve I felt immense;
Today I feel like thirty cents.
My eyes are bleared, my coppers hot
I'd like to eat but I cannot!
It is no time for mirth and laughter—
The cold, gray dawn of the morning after.

If ever I want to sign the pledge,
It's the morning after I've had an edge;
When I've been full of the oil of joy
And fancied I was a sporty boy.
The world was one kaleidoscope
Of purple bliss, transcendent hope,
But now I'm feeling mighty blue—
Three cheers for the W.C.T.U.
R-E-M-O-R-S-E!
Those dry Martinis did the work for me;
A dark brown taste, a burning thirst,
A head that's ready to split and burst,
I'd like to hold it under a pump;
When I hear a noise I want to jump.
It is no time for mirth and laughter—
The cold, gray dawn of the morning after.

—*George Ade.*

85

THE BOYS OF COLD WATER

"It is a pity," said John Wesley, "that the devil should have all of the good songs." Much as they might deplore the fact, foes of the liquor traffic were never able to compete lyrically with the boys in the back room. Their impeccable refrains lacked, somehow, the spark and sparkle that characterized many a roundelay dedicated to the Demon Rum. The example printed here is from that celebrated Temperance songster, *Cold Water Melodies.*

Oh! the boys of cold water are stout, hearty blades,
They drink not of Alchy, but from the cool shades—
They are lively and active, and always desire

To make mirth, glee and comfort, at each social fire,
And home to their dwellings in peace they retire.

Oh! the boys of cold water, how majestic they move
Thro' this vast land of freedom, of friendship and love.
Oh! wherever you meet them in their faces you'll see,
An expression of joy and of great harmony,
Oh! of all draughts of nature, cold water for me.

Oh! the boys of cold water, how persuasive they speak,
The tales of their past life, which makes our hearts ache
How they excite our feelings, and make us resign
The quaffing of brandy, of beer, ale and wine,
And pledge us forever to Temperance divine.

Oh! the boys of cold water are inspirited on
To the grand march of freedom, by the daughters of song,
Whose sweet intonations and bewitching strains
Have converted the drunkard, and given him means
To conquer old Alchy and dissunder his chains.

Then come up, my friends, to the altar of fame,
And there swear allegiance to the Goddess whose name
Is Temperance, which causes your body and mind
To be strengthen'd and your pathway with pleasure en-
    twin'd,
Sweet Temperance, shed thy blessings o'er all mankind.

86

When Father Time swings round his scythe,
Intomb me 'neath the bounteous vine,
So that its juices red and blythe,
May cheer these thirsty bones of mine.
                    —*Eugene Field.*

87

THE EPICURE

Underneath this myrtle shade,
On flowery beds supinely laid,
With odorous oils my head o'erflowing,
And around it roses growing,
What should I do but drink away
The heat and troubles of the day?
In this more than kingly state,
Love himself shall on me wait.
Fill to me, Love; nay, fill it up;
And mingled cast into the cup
Wit, and mirth, and noble fires,
Vigorous health, and gay desires.
The wheel of life no less will stay
In a smooth than rugged way:
Since it equally doth flee,
Let the motion pleasant be.
Why do we precious ointments shower?
Nobler wines why do we pour?
Beauteous flowers why do we spread
Upon the monuments of the dead?
Nothing they but dust can show,
Or bones that hasten to be so.
Crown me with roses whilst I live,—
Now your wines and ointments give;
After death I nothing crave;
Let me alive my pleasures have!
All are Stoics in the grave.

—Abraham Cowley.

88

THE DEAD HOST'S WELCOME

'Tis late and cold; stir up the fire;
Sit close, and draw the table nigher;
Be merry, and drink wine that's old,
A hearty medicine 'gainst a cold:
Your beds of wanton down the best,
Where you shall tumble to your rest;
I could wish you wenches too,
But I am dead, and cannot do.
Call for the best the house may ring,
Sack, white, and claret, let them bring,
And drink apace, while breath you have;
You'll find but cold drink in the grave:
Plover, partridge for your dinner,
And a capon for the sinner,
You shall find ready when you're up,
And your horse shall have his sup:
Welcome, welcome, shall fly round,
And I shall smile, though under ground.

—*John Fletcher.*

VI

THE MINSTREL STAG

The man that hath no music in himself,

Nor is not mov'd with concord of sweet sounds,

Is fit for treasons, stratagems, and spoils;

The motions of his spirit are dull as night,

And his affections dark as Erebus:

Let no such man be trusted.

—*Shakespeare.*

89

FRANKIE AND JOHNNIE

Of the making of *Frankie and Johnnie* verses, there is no end. The first vague outline dates back nearly a century. All of the variations, placed end to end, reach this common conclusion: (a) There was a Frankie; (b) there was a Johnnie; (c) he done her wrong; (d) she shot her man. Upon this skeleton framework one may erect as elaborate a ballad as fancy and discretion dictate.

Actually there is no authentic version of *Frankie and Johnnie*. For the form presented here we are deeply indebted to Sigmund Spaeth, who has labored diligently gathering fragments from many sources. However, the present editor, not to be outdone by custom, has made certain alterations and interpolations on his own account.

Frankie and Johnnie were lovers,
O-my-gawd how they did love,
They swore to be true to each other,
Just as true as the stars up above
    He was her man,
    But he done her wrong.

Frankie she was a good woman,
Just like everyone knows,
She'd give her man a hundred dollars,
Just to buy himself a suit of clothes,
    He was her man,
    But he done her wrong.

Frankie and Johnnie went walking,
Johnnie in his brand-new suit,
"O-my-gawd," said Frankie,
"But don't my Johnnie look cute?"

109

He was her man,
But he done her wrong.

Frankie went down to Memphis,
She went on the morning train,
She paid a hundred dollars,
For Johnnie a watch and chain,
  He was her man,
  But he done her wrong.

Frankie lived down in a crib-house,
Crib-house with only two doors,
Gave all her money to Johnnie,
He spent it on those parlor-girls,
  He was her man,
  But he done her wrong.

Frankie went down to the corner,
Just for a bucket of beer,
She said, "Oh, Mr. Bartender,
Has my lovin' Johnnie been here?
  He is my man,
  And he wouldn't do me wrong."

"I don't want to cause you no trouble,
I don't want to tell you no lie,
But I saw your lover half an hour ago,
With a girl named Nellie Bly.
  He is your man,
  But he's done you wrong."

Frankie went down to the pawn-shop,
She bought herself a little forty-four,
She aimed it at the ceiling,

And shot a big hole in the floor,
   "Where is my man?
   He's doing me wrong."

Frankie went down to the Chippie Joint;
She rang that great big bell.
"Stand back, all of you chippies,
Or I'll blow you all to hell.
   I want my man,
   He's doin' me wrong."

Frankie looked over the transom,
And there to her great surprise,
Yes, there on the bed sat Johnnie,
A lovin' up Nellie Bly.
   He was her man,
   But he done her wrong.

Frankie threw back her kimono,
She took out the little forty-four,
Roota-toot-toot, three times she did shoot,
Right through the hardwood door,
   She shot her man,
   Because he done her wrong.

"Roll me over easy,
Roll me over slow,
Roll me over easy, boys,
'Cause my wounds they hurt me so.
   But I was your man,
   And I done you wrong."

"Bring out your rubber-tired carriage,
Bring out your rubber-tired hack,

I'm goin' to take my man to the cemetery,
And I ain't a-goin' to bring him back,
  For he was my man,
  And he done me wrong.

"Oh, bring 'round a thousand policemen,
Bring 'em around to-day,
To lock me in that dungeon,
And throw the key away,
  I shot my man,
  'Cause he done me wrong.

"Yes, put me in that dungeon,
Oh, put me in that cell,
Put me where the northeast wind
Blows from the southwest corner of hell,
  I shot my man,
  'Cause he done me wrong.

"I've saved up a little bit of money,
I'll save up a little bit more,
I'll send it all to his widow,
And say it's from the woman next door.
  He was my man,
  But he done me wrong."

Frankie went to his coffin,
She looked down on his face,
She said "O Lord, have mercy on me,
I wish I could take his place.
  He was my man,
  But he done me wrong."

Frankie she heard a rumbling,
Away down in the ground,
Perhaps it was little Johnnie,
Where she had shot him down,
  He was her man,
  But he done her wrong.

Johnnie he was a gambler,
He gambled for the gain,
The very last words he ever said
Were "High, low, jack, and the game."
  He was her man,
  But he done her wrong.

Frankie she said to the warden,
"What are they goin' to do?"
The warden he said to Frankie,
"It's the electric chair for you.
  You shot your man,
  Though he done you wrong."

The sheriff came 'round in the morning,
And said it was all for the best,
He said her lover Johnnie
Was nothin' but a gawdam pest.
  He was her man,
  But he done her wrong.

The judge said to the jury,
"It's as plain as plain can be.
This woman shot her lover.
It's murder in the second degree.
  He was her man,
  But he done her wrong."

Now it was not murder in the second degree,
And was not murder in the third,
This woman simply dropped her man
Like a hunter drops a bird.
    He was her man,
    But he done her wrong.

Frankie she sits in the parlor,
Underneath the electric fan,
Telling her little grandchildren
To beware of the gawdam man,
    "He'll do you wrong,
    Just as sure as you're born."

This story has no moral,
This story has no end,
This story only goes to show
That there ain't no good in men,
    He was her man,
    And he done her wrong.

90

CASEY JONES

Engineer John Luther Jones, called "Casey" because he hailed from Cayce, Ky. (not Kansas City, as often reported), made his historic run on the night of April 29, 1900, the fatal wreck occurring in the early morning hours, near Vaughn, Miss.

Wallace Saunders, Negro engine wiper at Jackson, Tenn., following a custom common in railroading, concocted a few crude verses, telling the tale of Casey and his fate. A couple of years later T. Lawrence Seibert and Eddie Newton took the basic material, moved the locale westward, and fashioned the song, substantially as it is now sung. The common assertion that Seibert and Newton were railroad men is an error; they were professional song-writers. In this instance they apparently leaned heavily on a much older ballad, known as *Vanderbilt's Daughter*.

Incidentally, Casey's conductor, Chap Turner, died of natural causes, at the age of 72, as this manuscript was being prepared for the printer.

Come all you rounders if you want to hear,
A story about a brave Engineer,
Casey Jones was the rounder's name
On a six eight wheeler, boys, he won his fame.
The caller called Casey at a half past four,
Kissed his wife at the station door,
Mounted to the cabin with his orders in his hand,
And he took his farewell trip to that promised land.

CHORUS

Casey Jones! Mounted to the cabin,
Casey Jones! With his orders in his hand,
Casey Jones! Mounted to the cabin
And he took his farewell trip to that promised land.

Put in your water and shovel in your coal,
Put your head out the window, watch them drivers roll,
I'll run her till she leaves the rail,
'Cause I'm eight hour late with that western mail.
He looked at his watch and his watch was slow,
He looked at the water and the water was low,
He turned to the Fireman and he said,
"We're going to reach Frisco but we'll all be dead."

CHORUS

Casey Jones! Going to reach Frisco,
Casey Jones! But we'll all be dead.
Casey Jones! Going to reach Frisco,
We're going to reach Frisco, but we'll all be dead.

Casey pulled up that Reno hill,
He tooted for the crossing with an awful shrill,
The switchman knew by the engine's moan
That the man at the throttle was Casey Jones.
He pulled up within two miles of the place,
Number four stared him right in the face,
Turned to the Fireman, said, "Boy, you'd better jump,
'Cause there's two locomotives that's a-going to bump."

CHORUS

Casey Jones! Two locomotives!
Casey Jones! That's a-going to bump!
Casey Jones! Two locomotives!
There's two locomotives that's a-going to bump.

Casey said just before he died,
"There's two more roads that I'd like to ride."
Fireman said, "What could that be?"
"The Southern Pacific and the Santa Fe."
Mrs. Jones sat on her bed a-sighing,
Just received a message that Casey was dying,
Said "Go to bed, children, and hush your crying,
'Cause you got another papa on the Salt Lake Line." [1]

[1] Sigmund Spaeth remarks, "It seems there were *two* Irishmen . . ." However, Widow Jones (who never re-married) insists that the implication is a base and baseless libel.

CHORUS

Mrs. Casey Jones! Got another papa!
Mrs. Casey Jones! On that Salt Lake Line!
Mrs. Casey Jones! Got another Papa!
And you've got another Papa on that Salt Lake Line.

91

THE FACE ON THE BARROOM FLOOR

This classic, by Hugh D'Arcy, was first printed in 1887, and titled *The Face Upon the Floor*. It is amusing to note that it was never intended to point out the perils of strong drink, but merely to portray the degradation of an artist tortured by the loss of his sweetheart. The poem was seized by the W.C.T.U., and later the Anti-Saloon League, the title altered, and millions of copies distributed as propaganda.

"If I thought my poem had done anything to help Prohibition," said D'Arcy, in 1925, "I would go take a running jump into the Hudson."

The poem follows the familiar "my-pal-stole-my-gal" theme. The artist, "gone gutter," drifts into a barroom, begging a drink. Fortified by a swig of whiskey, he tells his tale in too-many verses.

'Twas a balmy summer evening, and a goodly crowd was
    there,
Which well-nigh filled Joe's barroom, on the corner of the
    square;
And as songs and witty stories came through the open door,
A vagabond crept slowly in and posed upon the floor.

"Where did it come from?" someone said. "The wind has
    blown it in."
"What does it want?" another cried. "Some whiskey, rum
    or gin?"

"Here, Toby, sic 'em, if your stomach's equal to the work—
I wouldn't touch him with a fork, he's filthy as a Turk."

This badinage the poor wretch took with stoical good grace;
In fact, he smiled as tho' he thought he'd struck the proper
    place.
"Come, boys, I know there's kindly hearts among so good
    a crowd—
To be in such good company would make a deacon proud.

"Give me a drink—that's what I want—I'm out of funds,
    you know,
When I had cash to treat the gang this hand was never slow.
What? You laugh as if you thought this pocket never held
    a sou;
I once was fixed as well, my boys, as any one of you.

"There, thanks, that's braced me nicely; God bless you one
    and all;
Next time I pass this good saloon I'll make another call.
Give you a song? No, I can't do that; my singing days are
    past;
My voice is cracked, my throat's worn out, and my lungs are
    going fast.

"I'll tell you a funny story, and a fact, I promise, too.
Say! Give me another whiskey, and I'll tell you what I'll do—
That I was ever a decent man not one of you would think;
But I was, some four or five years back. Say, give me an-
    other drink.

"Fill her up, Joe, I want to put some life into my frame—
Such little drinks to a bum like me are miserably tame;

Five fingers—there, that's the scheme—and corking whiskey,
    too.
Well, here's luck, boys, and landlord, my best regards to you.

"You've treated me pretty kindly and I'd like to tell you how
I came to be the dirty sot you see before you now.
As I told you, once I was a man, with muscle, frame, and
    health,
And but for a blunder ought to have made considerable
    wealth.

"I was a painter—not one that daubed on bricks and wood,
But an artist, and for my age, was rated pretty good.
I worked hard at my canvas, and was bidding fair to rise,
For gradually I saw the star of fame before my eyes.

"I made a picture perhaps you've seen, 'tis called the 'Chase
    of Fame.'
It brought me fifteen hundred pounds and added to my
    name,
And then I met a woman—now comes the funny part—
With eyes that petrified my brain, and sunk into my heart.

"Why don't you laugh? 'Tis funny that the vagabond you see
Could ever love a woman, and expect her love for me;
But 'twas so, and for a month or two, her smiles were freely
    given,
And when her loving lips touched mine, it carried me to
    Heaven.

"Boys, did you ever see a girl for whom your soul you'd give,
With a form like the Milo Venus, too beautiful to live;
With eyes that would beat the Koh-i-noor, and a wealth of
    chestnut hair?
If so, 'twas she, for there never was another half so fair.

"I was working on a portrait, one afternoon in May,
Of a fair-haired boy, a friend of mine, who lived across the
    way.
And Madeline admired it, and much to my surprise,
Said she'd like to know the man that had such dreamy eyes.

"It didn't take long to know him, and before the month had
    flown
My friend had stole my darling, and I was left alone;
And ere a year of misery had passed above my head,
The jewel I had treasured so had tarnished and was dead.

"That's why I took to drink, boys. Why, I never see you
    smile,
I thought you'd be amused, and laughing all the while.
Why, what's the matter, friend? There's a tear-drop in your
    eye,
Come, laugh like me. 'Tis only babes and women that should
    cry.

"Say, boys, if you give me just another whiskey I'll be glad,
And I'll draw right here a picture of the face that drove me
    mad.
Give me that piece of chalk with which you mark the base-
    ball score—
You shall see the lovely Madeline upon the barroom floor."

Another drink, and with chalk in hand, the vagabond began
To sketch a face that well might buy the soul of any man.
Then, as he placed another lock upon the shapely head,
With a fearful shriek, he leaped and fell across the picture—
    dead.

                              —*H. Antoine D'Arcy.*

92

THE BALLAD OF YUKON JAKE

(The Hermit of Shark Tooth Shoal)

Oh the North Countree is a hard countree
  That mothers a bloody brood;
And its icy arms hold hidden charms
  For the greedy, the sinful and lewd.

And strong men rust, from the gold and lust
  That sears the Northland soul,
But the wickedest born, from the pole to the Horn,
  Is the Hermit of Shark Tooth Shoal.

Now Jacob Kaime was the Hermit's name,
  In the days of his pious youth,
Ere he cast a smirch on the Baptist church
  By betraying a girl named Ruth.

But now men quake at Yukon Jake,
  The Hermit of Shark Tooth Shoal,
For that is the name that Jacob Kaime
  Is known by from Nome to the Pole.

He was just a boy and the parson's joy
  (Ere he fell for the gold and the muck),
And he learned to pray, with the hogs and hay
  On a farm near Keokuk.

But a Service tale of illicit kale—
  And whiskey and women wild—
Drained the morals clean as a soup-tureen
  From this poor but honest child.

He longed for the bite of a Yukon night
    And the Northern Light's weird flicker,
For a game of stud in the frozen mud,
    And the taste of raw red licker.

He wanted to mush along in the slush
    With a team of huskie hounds,
And to fire his gat at a beaver hat
    And knock it out of bounds.

So he left his home for the hell-town Nome
    On Alaska's ice-ribbed shores,
And he learned to curse and to drink and worse—
    Till the rum dripped from his pores.

When the boys on a spree were drinking it free
    In a Malamute saloon
And Dan McGrew and his dangerous crew
    Shot craps with the piebald coon:

When the Kid on his stool banged away like a fool
    At a jag-time melody
And the bar-keep vowed to the hardboiled crowd
    That he'd cree-mate Sam McGee—

Then Jacob Kaime, who had taken the name
    Of Yukon Jake, the Killer,
Would rake the dive with his forty-five
    Till the atmosphere grew chiller.

With a sharp command he'd make 'em stand
    And deliver their hard-earned dust,
Then drink the bar dry of rum and rye,
    As a Klondike bully must.

Without coming to blows he would tweak the nose
  Of Dangerous Dan McGrew
And becoming bolder, throw over his shoulder
  The Lady that's known as Lou.

Oh, tough as steak was Yukon Jake—
  Hardboiled as a picnic egg.
He washed his shirt in the Klondike dirt,
  And drank his rum by the keg.

In fear of their lives (or because of their wives)
  He was shunned by the best of his pals;
An outcast he, from the comraderie
  Of all but wild animals.

So he bought him the whole of Shark Tooth Shoal,
  A reef in the Bering Sea,
And he lived by himself on a sea lion's shelf
  In lonely iniquity.

But miles away, in Keokuk, Ia.
  Did a ruined maiden fight
To remove the smirch from the Baptist Church
  By bringing the heathen Light.

And the Elders declared that all would be squared
  If she carried the holy words
From her Keokuk home to the hell-town Nome
  To save those sinful birds.

So, two weeks later, she took a freighter,
  For the gold-cursed land near the Pole,
But Heaven ain't made for a lass that betrayed—
  She was wrecked on Shark Tooth Shoal!

All hands were tossed in the sea and lost—
    All but the maiden Ruth,
Who swam to the edge of the sea lion's ledge
    Where abode the love of her youth.

He was hunting a seal for his evening meal
    (He handled a mean harpoon)
When he saw at his feet not something to eat,
    But a girl in a frozen swoon.

Whom he dragged to his lair by her dripping hair,
    And he rubbed her knees with gin.
To his surprise she opened her eyes
    And revealed—his Original Sin!

His eight months' beard grew stiff and weird
    And it felt like a chestnut burr,
And he swore by his gizzard—and the Arctic blizzard
    That he'd do right by her.

But the cold sweat froze on the end of her nose
    Till it gleamed like a Tecla pearl,
While her bright hair fell like a flame from hell
    Down the back of the grateful girl.

But a hopeless rake was Yukon Jake
    The Hermit of Shark Tooth Shoal!
And the dizzy maid he rebetrayed
    And wrecked her immortal soul!

Then he rowed her ashore with a broken oar,
    And he sold her to Dan McGrew
For a huskie dog and a hot egg-nog—
    As rascals are wont to do.

Now ruthless Ruth is a maid uncouth
  With scarlet cheeks and lips,
And she sings rough songs to the drunken throngs
  That come from the sealing ships.

For a rouge-stained kiss from this infamous miss
  They will give a seal's sleek fur,
Or perhaps a sable, if they are able;
  It's much the same to her. . . .

Oh, the North Countree is a hard countree,
  That mothers a bloody brood;
And its icy arms hold hidden charms
  For the greedy, the sinful and lewd.

And strong men rust, from the gold and lust
  That sears the Northland soul,
But the wickedest born from the Pole to the Horn
  Is the Hermit of Shark Tooth Shoal!

                                    —*Edward E. Paramore, Jr.*

93

CASEY AT THE BAT

As you well know, this is the poem that De Wolf Hopper made famous, through innumerable recitals. Or would it, perhaps, be more to the point to say that the poem made Hopper famous? In any case, we have rather lost sight of the fact that the ballad was foundationed in fact. There *was* a Mighty Casey—indeed there yet is, for he is still living in Washington, D.C. Mr. Casey, luminary of a minor league at the turn of the century, declares that in the poem Author Thayer has much maligned him. He was, he is careful to explain, a pitcher—and was never supposed to hit:

It looked extremely rocky for the Mudville nine that day,
The score stood four to six with but an inning left to play.
And so, when Cooney died at first, and Burrows did the same,
A pallor wreathed the features of the patrons of the game.
A straggling few got up to go, leaving there the rest,
With that hope which springs eternal within the human breast.
For they thought if only Casey could get a whack at that,
They'd put up even money with Casey at the bat.
But Flynn preceded Casey, and likewise so did Blake,
And the former was a pudding and the latter was a fake;
So on that stricken multitude a death-like silence sat,
For there seemed but little chance of Casey's getting to the bat.
But Flynn let drive a single to the wonderment of all,
And the much despised Blakey tore the cover off the ball,
And when the dust had lifted and they saw what had occurred,
There was Blakey safe on second, and Flynn a-hugging third.
Then from the gladdened multitude went up a joyous yell,
It bounded from the mountain top and rattled in the dell,
It struck upon the hillside, and rebounded on the flat,
For Casey, mighty Casey, was advancing to the bat.
There was ease in Casey's manner as he stepped into his place,
There was pride in Casey's bearing and a smile on Casey's face,
And when responding to the cheers he lightly doffed his hat,
No stranger in the crowd could doubt, 'twas Casey at the bat.
Ten thousand eyes were on him as he rubbed his hands with dirt,

Five thousand tongues applauded as he wiped them on his
    shirt;
And while the writhing pitcher ground the ball into his hip—
Defiance gleamed from Casey's eye—a sneer curled Casey's
    lip.
And now the leather-covered sphere came hurtling through
    the air,
And Casey stood a-watching it in haughty grandeur there;
Close by the sturdy batsman the ball unheeded sped—
"That hain't my style," said Casey—"Strike one," the Umpire
    said.
From the bleachers black with people there rose a sullen
    roar,
Like the beating of the storm waves on a stern and distant
    shore,
"Kill him! kill the Umpire!" shouted some one from the
    stand—
And it's likely they'd have done it had not Casey raised his
    hand.
With a smile of Christian charity great Casey's visage shone,
He stilled the rising tumult and he bade the game go on;
He signalled to the pitcher and again the spheroid flew,
But Casey still ignored it and the Umpire said "Strike two."
"Fraud!" yelled the maddened thousands, and the echo an-
    swered "Fraud."
But one scornful look from Casey and the audience was
    awed;
They saw his face grow stern and cold; they saw his muscles
    strain,
And they knew that Casey would not let that ball go by
    again.
The sneer is gone from Casey's lip; his teeth are clenched
    with hate,

He pounds with cruel violence his bat upon the plate;
And now the pitcher holds the ball, and now he lets it go,
And now the air is shattered by the force of Casey's blow.
Oh! somewhere in this favored land the sun is shining bright,
The band is playing somewhere, and somewhere hearts are
  light.
And somewhere men are laughing, and somewhere children
  shout;
But there is no joy in Mudville—mighty Casey has "Struck
Out."

—*Ernest Lawrence Thayer.*

94

HINKY DINKY

(Or, if you prefer, "Mademoiselle From Armentières")

Through all time the infantry has produced more songs
than any other branch of the service. For men who march
must sing. And *Hinky Dinky* stands as the American dough-
boy's song of songs, its verses as countless as the stars—and
as luminously bright.

The original *Hinky Dinky* verses concerned the osculatory
desires and frustrations of a certain *Mademoiselle* who hailed
from Armentières. No linguistic purists, the doughboys rhymed
the historic locale with "years," giving the word three sylla-
bles, thus—"Ar-men-*teers*" :

Oh, Mademoiselle from Armentières,
  Parley voo.
Oh, Mademoiselle from Armentières,
  Parley voo.
Oh, Mademoiselle from Armentières,
She ain't been kissed for forty years.
  Hinky, Dinky, parley voo.

Innumerable verses were concocted to commemorate the events of a march, or as an outlet for a soldier's momentary peeve. Each group had its own particular favorites. One series, I recall, had to do with the romantic adventures of the *Mademoiselle* and the *Little Marine*. In one version, a concluding couplet informs us that

> The Little Marine he grew and grew,
> And now he's part of the army too.

Sometimes the ballad would sound a distinctly utilitarian note,

> Oh, farmer, have you a daughter fair,
> Who can wash a soldier's underwear?

Or now and then he would voice his suspicion of the Frenchman and his wily ways,

> Oh, the Frogs they are a funny race,
> They swipe the eye-teeth from your face.

Naturally enough, the soldier in the ranks did not overlook an opportunity to vent his antipathy to those in High Places, when the lambasting could be done discreetly in song. To the *Hinky Dinky* tune the doughboys sang with huge delight:

> The General got the *Croix de Guerre*,
> But the son of a gun, he was never there.

Or again:

> The officers get all the steak,
> And all we get is the belly-ache.

With prophetic accuracy, the song concludes:

You may forget the gas and shell,
You'll never forget the Mademoiselle!

It was that irrepressible soldier, Charles MacArthur (subsequently co-author of *The Front Page;* now a motion picture impresario) who, being enjoined by a superior officer to "whip them goddam punks int' form," drilled perhaps the toughest group of eggs in the A.E.F. to the somewhat surprising tune of *Jesus Wants Me for a Sunbeam.* And to this air they marched for the duration of hostilities.

95

JIM BLUDSO

Wal, no! I can't tell whar he lives,
    Because he don't live, you see;
Leastways, he's got out of the habit
    Of livin' like you and me.
Where have you been for the last three years
    That you haven't heard folks tell
How Jemmy Bludso passed-in his checks,
    The night of the Prairie Belle?

He weren't no saint—them engineers
    Is all pretty much alike—
One wife in Natchez-under-the-Hill,
    And another one here in Pike.
A keerless man in his talk was Jim,
    And an awkward man in a row—
But he never flunked, and he never lied;
    I reckon he never knowed how.

And this was all the religion he had—
    To treat his engines well;

Never be passed on the river;
  To mind the pilot's bell;
And if ever the Prairie Belle took fire,
  A thousand times he swore,
He'd hold her nozzle agin the bank
  Till the last soul got ashore.

All boats have their day on the Mississip,
  And her day come at last.
The Movastar was a better boat,
  But the Belle she wouldn't be passed;
And so come tearin' along that night,—
  The oldest craft on the line,
With a nigger squat on her safety valve,
  And her furnace crammed, rosin and pine.

The fire bust out as she clared the bar,
  And burnt a hole in the night,
And quick as a flash she turned, and made
  To that willer-bank on the right.
There was runnin' and cursin', but Jim yelled out
  Over all the infernal roar,
"I'll hold her nozzle agin the bank
  Till the last galoot's ashore."

Through the hot black breath of the burnin' boat
  Jim Bludso's voice was heard,
And they all had trust in his cussedness,
  And knowed he would keep his word.
And, sure's you're born, they all got off
  Afore the smokestacks fell,—
And Bludso's ghost went up alone
  In the smoke of the Prairie Belle.

He weren't no saint—but at jedgment
  I'd run my chance with Jim,
'Longside of some pious gentlemen
  That wouldn't shook hands with him.
He'd seen his duty, a dead-sure thing—
  And went for it thar and then:
And Christ ain't a going to be too hard
  On a man that died for men.

                —*John Hay.*

96

LITTLE JOE, THE WRANGLER

The present editor heard and sang "Little Joe" for twenty years or more with no accurate knowledge of its origin. However, Jack Thorp, of New Mexico, deposes and states that he wrote the song in 1898, and it appears in his *Songs of the Cowboys.* Several versions are extant, but the one printed below is the author's own. Explanatory notes are our contribution.

This selection is typical of the plains, since the cowboy treasures a strong lugubrious streak, and dearly delights in the doleful ballad.

It's little Joe, the wrangler, he'll wrangle nevermore,
His days with the *remuda* [1] they are o'er;
'Twas a year ago last April he rode into our camp,—
Just a little Texas stray and all alone,—

It was late in the evening he rode up to our herd
On a little Texas pony he called "Chaw."
With his brogan shoes and ov'ralls, a tougher lookin' kid
You never in your life before had saw.

[1] A Spanish collective term denoting saddle horses from which the day's mounts are chosen.

His saddle was a Texas "kack," [2] built many years ago,
With an O. K. spur on one foot lightly swung;
His "hot roll" in a cotton sack so loosely tied behind,
And his canteen from his saddle-horn was swung.

He said that he had to leave home, his pa had married twice;
And his new ma whipped him every day or two;
So he saddled up old Chaw one night and lit a shuck this
    way,
And he's now trying to paddle his own canoe.

He said if we would give him work, he'd do the best he could,
Though he didn't know straight up about a cow;
So the boss he cut out a mount and kindly put him on,
For he sorta liked this little kid somehow;

Learned him to wrangle horses and to try to know them all,
And get them in at daylight if he could;
To follow the chuck-wagon and always hitch the team,
And to help the *cocinero* rustle wood.

We had driven to the Pecos, the weather being fine;
We had camped on the south side in a bend;
When a norther commenced blowin', we had doubled up our
    guard,
For it taken all of us to hold them in.

Little Joe, the wrangler, was called out with the rest;
Though the kid had scarcely reached the herd,
When the cattle they stampeded, like a hailstorm long they
    fled,
Then we were all a-ridin' for the lead.

[2] A cheap, run-of-mine saddle, for which the cowboy has great contempt.

'Midst the streaks of lightnin' a horse we could see in the
    lead,
'Twas Little Joe, the wrangler, in the lead;
He was riding Old Blue Rocket with a slicker o'er his head,
A-tryin' to check the cattle in their speed.

At last we got them milling and kinda quieted down,
And the extra guard back to the wagon went;
But there was one a-missin' and we knew it at a glance,
'Twas our little Texas stray, poor Wrangling Joe.

The next morning just at daybreak, we found where Rocket
    fell,
Down in a washout twenty feet below;
And beneath the horse, mashed to a pulp,—his spur had rung
    the knell,—
Was our little Texas stray, poor Wrangling Joe.
                                                —*Jack Thorp.*

97

SAM BASS

Like many another folk song, *Sam Bass* has a sound histori-
cal base. As the ballad recites in its initial verse, Bass was
born in Indiana and headed West at the age of seventeen. He
died of gun wounds on his twenty-seventh birthday anniver-
sary. But for one rip-roaring, hell-raising decade he contrived
to be quite a thorn in the sides of sundry Texas Rangers.
Asked on his deathbed by officers of the law to name his associates, Bass scornfully replied: "If a man knows any secrets,
he should die and go to hell with them in him."

Sam Bass was born in Indiana, it was his native home,
And at the age of seventeen, young Sam began to roam.

Sam first came out to Texas a cowboy for to be—
A kinder-hearted fellow you seldom ever see.

Sam used to deal in race stock, one called the Denton mare;
He matched her in scrub races and took her to the fair.
Sam used to coin the money and spent it just as free,
He always drank good whiskey wherever he might be.

Sam left the Collins ranch in the merry month of May
With a herd of Texas cattle the Black Hills for to see,
Sold out in Custer City and then got on a spree—
A harder set of cowboys you seldom ever see.

On their way back to Texas they robbed the U. P. train,
And then split up in couples and started out again.
Joe Collins and his partner were overtaken soon,
With all their hard-earned money they had to meet their
   doom.

Sam made it back to Texas all right side up with care;
Rode into the town of Denton with all his friends to share.
Sam's life was short in Texas; three robberies did he do:
He robbed all the passenger, mail, and express cars too.

Sam had four companions—four bold and daring lads—
They were Richardson, Jackson, Joe Collins, and Old Dad;
Four more bold and daring cowboys the rangers never knew,
They whipped the Texas Rangers and ran the boys in blue.

Sam had another companion, called Arkansas for short,
Was shot by a Texas Ranger by the name of Thomas Floyd;

Oh, Tom is a big six-footer and thinks he's mighty fly,
But I can tell you his racket—he's a deadbeat on the sly.

Jim Murphy was arrested, and then released on bail;
He jumped his bond at Tyler and then took the train for
    Terrell;
But Mayor Jones had posted Jim and that was all a stall,
'Twas only a plan to capture Sam before the coming fall.

Sam met his fate at Round Rock, July the twenty-first,
They pierced poor Sam with rifle balls and emptied out his
    purse.
Poor Sam he is a corpse and six foot under clay,
And Jackson's in the bushes trying to get away.[1]

Jim had borrowed Sam's good gold and didn't want to pay,
The only shot he saw was to give poor Sam away.
He sold out Sam and Barnes and left their friends to mourn—
Oh, what a scorching Jim will get when Gabriel blows his
    horn! [2]

And so he sold out Sam and Barnes and left their friends to
    mourn.
Oh, what a scorching Jim will get when Gabriel blows his
    horn!
Perhaps he's got to heaven, there's none of us can say,
But if I'm right in my surmise he's gone the other way.

----

[1] Jackson did, indeed, get away, and was never heard from thereafter.
Bass, realizing his wounds must prove fatal, gave Jackson his race horse and
urged his partner to "run for it."
[2] There is testimony to the effect that Sam's friends subsequently slipped
a deadly poison in Murphy's eye medicine, causing him to die a raving
maniac.

98
THE LOVESICK COWBOY

If there is, anywhere in the balladry of the West, a record of a cowboy winning and holding the love of a Good Woman, the instance at the moment escapes the recollection of your editor. *The Lovesick Cowboy* is typical of dozens of plaintive folk songs, each concluding with the inevitable "take warning and heed what I say":

I am a bold cowboy, from Midland I came,
But my virtue's departed, I'm covered with shame;
The cold darts of Cupid have wrought me much grief,
My heart's burst asunder, I can find no relief.

I am a bold cowboy, on the green prairies roam,
My name is engraved on the sand hills alone;
In the town of Odessa I am very well known
As a dashing young cowboy, and Midland's my home.

But I will tell you my troubles without further delay,
Of a sweet little lassie who my heart stole away;
She was a good woman's daughter upon the north side,
And I always intended to make her my bride.

But one Sabbath morning a letter I received,
She said from her promise she long had deceived;
She would marry another, she long had delayed,
And the next time I met her she would no more be a maid.

Come all you young cowboys, I'm tellin' you true,
Don't depend on a woman—you're beat if you do;
And when you meet one with bright golden hair,
Just think of this cowboy that will die in despair.

Kind friends, take warning and heed what I say,
For the message of death is calling today;
How soon you will follow there is no one can tell;
I ask God to help you and bid you farewell.

99

"PREACHER DUNN," THE OUTLAW HORSE

"Powder River" Lee derives his name from his habitat
along the celebrated stream which runs from southern Wyoming into central Montana. It affords inspiration for the cowboy yell, "Powder River, let 'er buck! She's a mile wide, an
inch deep—full o' dust and flatfish—swimmin' holes fer grass-
hoppers. Cross 'er anywhere! Yeou-uhh—Yippee!—she rolls
up hill from Texas."

Of *Preacher Dunn* "Powder River" Lee says: "He was a big
old rawboned bucking horse that was never ridden. There
were plenty such horses who never appeared in contests, but
were well known to range-riding cowboys. They generally
had their ears cut short, and were thus known as 'croppies'."
Preacher Dunn was famed all over Wyoming and Montana.
Later in his career, he broke his own neck and killed the
rider at Miles City, Montana.

The ballad appears in a collection published by "Powder
River" Lee under title of *The Stampede:*

I heard about this outlaw, they called him Preacher Dunn,
And everybody knowed him claimed he was the devil's son.
I rides up to the O-Four Bar; a rancher, fixin' fence,
Says "How de do," and I replied, "I'm feelin' jest immense."
The air was crisp and tinglin' like, and the coulees full of
   snow,
And I was sure a-feelin' fine, although my wad was low.
He speaks up kind of easy like, "I reckon from yore style,
That you've been snappin' broncs and punchin' cattle for
   awhile."

I turned and looped my latigo, and reckoned he was right,
And mentions I was lookin' up some broncos for to fight—
He says, "I have an outlaw horse who bucks, and when he's
   through,
He keeps on percolatin' till he breaks hisself in two."
Now me, I'm all excited, and says, "What will you give
To rake this sack of bones until he looks like a sieve?"
He says, "You better stay tonight, and try to mount this one,
But I'm stakin' you to twenty you don't ride old Preacher
   Dunn."

"That's fair enough, old pardner, now, I reckon that's a bet.
The way I fork a croppy horse, I teach 'em how to sweat;
I rake 'em and I scratch 'em till the cows begin to weep;
And when they keep a-buckin' I jest ride 'em in my sleep."
We loaded my equipment, with my saddle in the rear,
And I goes on explainin' how to ride a Texas steer.
You leap upon him, grab his horns, and then begin to shout,
And if you steer him by his tail, you're bound to wear him
   out.

He busted out a-laffin' then we chatted fer awhile,
And ev'ry thing Ah said tuh him would always fetch a smile;
Ah lays that night a-dreamin' and Ah wakes up with a grin
And then Ah ambles out tuh teach this outlaw how tu spin.
Ah climbs inside the log corral, and standin' by a chute
Wuz Preacher Dunn, the outlaw, shore an ornery lookin'
   brute,
With snaky eyes and croppy ears, a-pinted tuh a tip,
The bosses' brand, an O-four-bar, a-planted on hees hip.

Square ol' forehead bulgin' high, wide-set roman nose,
Shoulders low-extendin' south, knocknees, pigeon toes,

Neck jest like a wether's, and a crooked hangin' jaw,
That outlaw shore descended frum an ornery maw-in-law.
Ah rolled mah quid and cinched mah belt and started
   through the gate;
Ah knowed Ah shore would hev tuh ride to earn that twenty
   straight.
I buckles on mah chaps and spurs, and picks me up mah
   twine,
Ah snaked mah way along the fence an' says, "Ol' boy, yore
   mine."

Ah piles mah loop around hees neck, 'twas shore a purty
   fight,
The blind comes next and then the saddle, cinched 'er good
   an' tight.
Ah leaps up on hees center and Ah shouts "Pull off the blind,
Git out from under, all yuh boys, and let the cuss unwind."
He leaps right up toward the sun, then doubles in a knot,
He leaves the earth behind him and he's foggin' like a shot.
Away he goes, hell-bent for space—a-pitchin' fer the fence,
The way he flew would make an eagle look like thirty cents.

He tried tuh snap hisself in two—he's buckin' high and wide,
Ah don't see how he ever kept frum sheddin' all hees hide;
That rancher shore wuz talkin' straight, this broncho wuz a
   peach;
Ah started grabbin' leather [1] and Ah stuck jest like a leech.
His head beneath his forelegs, his hind ones tuh the sun,
His belly does the hula and he's wiggling on the run,
He's swappin' ends way over here and sometimes over there,
And me? Ah'm like a batch of glue; Ah'm stickin' everywhere.

---

[1] To "grab leather" is to grip the horn of the saddle for support.

Ah reckon this ol' outlaw could turn out twenty fits,
He'd twist around on thirty cents and hand yuh back two bits
And me? Ah'm huggin rawhide, fer all that I am worth,
He's wound up like an eight-day clock an' six feet off the
  earth.
At last he makes a nose dive frum way up in the air,
He wiggles out from under me and leaves me hangin' there;
And when Ah hits the earth again, all bloody, achin', torn,
Ah'm cussin' each damned outlaw since they all of them wuz
  born.
The boss hands me fifty and he says 'twuz worth the fun
To watch a broncho buster separate frum Preacher Dunn.

—Jack H. ("Powder River") Lee.

100

LULU

Cowboy ballads represent, perhaps, the last stand of vocal
purity in these more or less United States. Whatever they
may lack in rhyme or meter, they are almost invariably on a
High Moral Plane. In this respect, Lulu is somewhat of a
maverick. It is frankly a rambling rowdy-dowdy, sung with
great verve and feeling. While the verses that follow are
moderately respectable, some versions are highly unprint-
able. In justice to the cowboy, however, your editor must admit that he has more often encountered *Lulu* in the cities
than on the plains.

> If you don't quit monkeying with my Lulu,
> I'll tell you what I'll do,
> I'll carve you up with my bowie knife
> And shoot you with my pistol, too,
> And shoot you with my pistol, too.

My Lulu had a baby,
'Twas born on Christmas Day;
She washed its face in brandy
And called it Henry Clay,
And called it Henry Clay.

You know you couldn't gamble,
You ought to stay at home
And pick up chips for your mamma,
And let the gamblers alone,
And let the gamblers alone.

I seen my Lulu in the springtime,
I seen her in the fall;
She wrote me a letter in the winter-time,
Says, "Good-by, honey"—that's all,
Says, "Good-by, honey"—that's all.

My Lulu, she's a dandy,
She stands and drinks like a man,
She calls for gin and brandy,
And she doesn't give a damn,
And she doesn't give a damn.

I ain't goin' to work on the railroad,
I ain't goin' to lie in jail,
I'm goin' down to Cheyenne town
To live with my Lulu gal,
To live with my Lulu gal.

My Lulu hugged and kissed me,
She wrung my hand and cried;
She said I was the sweetest thing

That ever lived or died,
That ever lived or died.

Lulu had twin babies,
Born on Christmas Day;
She mashed one's head with a rollin' pin,
The other one got away,
The other one got away.

101

WAY OUT WEST

'Twas good to live when all the range,
Without no fence and fuss,
Belonged in partnership with God,
The Government, and us.

With sky-line bounds from east to west,
With room to go and come,
I liked my fellow man best
When he was scattered some.

When my old soul hunts range and rest
Beyond the last divide,
Just plant me on some strip of West
That's sunny, lone and wide.

Let cattle rub my headstone round,
And coyotes wail their kin,
Let hosses come and paw the mound,
But don't you fence it in.

102

THE BALLAD OF CACTUS NELL

Cactus Nell, in the gaudy gown
Of a dance hall jade in a border town,
Had tried her wiles on a man who seemed
To read her smiles as he stood and dreamed;
He paid no heed to the tell-tale leer
Of the dance hall queen as she lingered near,
But turned and walked to another place
Removed from the taunt of her painted face.

The she-thing paled with a tang of hate
At the slight implied by his measured gait;
Each step seemed telling as words might say
He despised her breed and the tinseled way;
And she raged within as the dance hall clan
Observed the move of the silent man,
And she made a vow that the man would pay
For the public slight in the dance hall way.

A whispered word, and a hurried plan
Was told in the ears of Diamond Dan,
Who hitched the guns in the belt he wore,
As he wandered out on the dance hall floor;
He stopped a bit, as an idler would,
Quite close to the place where the stranger stood,
And Nell, with the hate of her creed and race,
Stepped close and spat in the tall man's face.

Then silence fell, and the place was still—
Like the stage scene set for a sudden kill—

As the stranger stood and calmly viewed
The leering face of the woman lewd;
Then his eyes were turned till they rested on
Her consort near with his six-guns drawn;
And a grin crept up on his thin, cold lips
And his hands rested calm on his holstered hips.

"I reckon," he said, "there has been a day
When a mother loved you in a mother's way,
An' I reckon she prayed as her baby grew
That she'd never be a thing like you;
And so for her, an' the child she bore,
I have only pity, an' nothin' more,
But as for you"—turning to Diamond Dan—
"I'm callin' you, hombre, man to man."

The call was quick as a lightning flash,
And the shots rang out in a single crash,
And Diamond Dan slumped down to the floor
As the stranger walked toward the open door;
And Cactus Nell stared into empty space,
The blood all gone from her throat and face,
And deep in her heart a something stirred,
And her pale lips moved, but no one heard.

Well, the fiddles still squeal in the border town,
And the faro wheels spin as the chips flop down,
And the old-timers look in vain for Nell,
One-time queen of the road house hell;
But stories are afloat, and the card sharps say
She's living in Butte in a humble way;
Married? Sure, and they say her man
Is the guy who called the play on Diamond Dan!

103

THE GIRL WITH THE BLUE VELVET BAND

The age and ancestry of this gem are hidden in the dim recesses of the past. For a quarter of a century or more it has been a prime favorite of the western cowhand. To this day he delights in reciting it with melodramatic flourish. There is a persistent tradition that the masterpiece was written by a prisoner, serving a life sentence in a western penitentiary. The version printed here is slightly condensed.

One evening while out for a ramble;
Here or there without thought or design,
I chanced on a young girl, tall and slender,
At the corner of Kearney and Pine.

On her face was the first flush of nature,
And her bright eyes seemed to expand;
While her hair fell in rich, brilliant masses,
Was entwined in a blue velvet band.

To a house of gentle ruination,
She invited me with a sweet smile;
She seemed so refined, gay, and charming
That I thought I would tarry awhile.

She then shared with me a collection
Of wines of an excellent brand,
And conversed in politest language;
The Girl with the Blue Velvet Band.

But what struck me the most was an object
Designed by an artistic hand;
'Twas the costly "lay-out" of a hop-fiend,
And that fiend was my Blue Velvet Band.

On a pile of soft robes and pillows;
She reclined, I declare, on the floor,
Then we both hit the pipe and I slumbered,
I ponder it o'er and o'er.

'Tis months since the craven arm grasped me,
And in bliss did my life glide away;
From opium to "dipping" and thieving,
She artfully led day by day.

One evening, coming home wet and dreary,
With the swag from a jewelry store,
I heard the soft voice of my loved one,
As I gently opened the door.

"If you'll give me a clue to convict him,"
Said a stranger, in tones soft and bland,
"You'll then prove to me that you love me,"
"It's a go," said my Blue Velvet Band.

Ah! How my heart filled with anger,
At woman, so fair, false, and vile,
And to think that I once true adored her
Brought to my lips a contemptible smile.

All ill-gotten gains we had squandered,
And my life was hers to command;
Betrayed and deserted for another—
Could this be my Blue Velvet Band?

Just a few moments before I was hunted
By the cops, who wounded me, too,
And my temper was none the sweetest,
As I swung myself into their view.

And the copper, not liking the glitter
Of the "44" Colt in my hand,
Hurriedly left through the window,
Leaving me with my Blue Velvet Band.

What happened to me I will tell you;
I was "ditched" for a desperate crime;
There was hell in a bank about midnight,
And my pal was shot down in his prime.

As a convict of hard reputation,
Ten years of hard grind did I land,
And I often thought of the pleasures
I had with my Blue Velvet Band.

Many months have passed since this happened,
And the story belongs to the past;
I forgave her, but just retribution
Claimed this fair but false one at last.

She slowly sank lower and lower,
Down through life's shifting sands,
Till finally she died in a hop joint,
This girl with the Blue Velvet Band.

If she had been true when I met her,
A bright future for us was in store,
For I was an able mechanic,
And honest and square to the core.

But as sages of old have contended,
What's decreed us mortals must stand;
So a grave in the potter's field ended
My romance with the Blue Velvet Band.

104

ANNIE BREEN

Come all ye men of Arkansas, a tale to you I'll sing,
Of Annie Breen from old Kaintuck who made the forest ring.
For sweeter gal and sweeter voice no man did ever know,
And well she loved a straight-limbed lad whose name was
    Texas Joe.

To meetin' she and Joe they went, and oh, her eyes did shine,
To see him full of manly strength, so clear and tall and fine.
To be his wife and helping hand she wanted as her fate,
But sad the story that befell as now I will relate.

One morn when birds were singin' an' the lilacs were abloom,
There came unto the little town and there he took a room,
A evil-hearted city man who said he'd made his stake,
And then it was that the serpent in the Paradise did wake.

At meetin' after prayers were said, sweet Ann sang clear and
    fine.
The stranger said upon knees, "That girl she must be mine."
So arm in arm they both walked home and wandered up and
    down,
Which caused the neighbors, who loved Ann, to shake their
    heads and frown.

He entered in and brought a stain on Annie Breen's fair life.
He told her that he loved the girl, would take her for his wife.
When Joe got wind how matters stood his heart was like a
    stone,
With ne'er a word of parting he went off to Texas alone.

Before a year in a shallow grave lay Annie and her child,
But when the tidings reached brave Joe's ears that lad went
almost wild.
He saddled up and cantered hard, and rode both long and
fast
And in Fort Smith he found the man who'd ruined Ann at
last.

Then words were spoke and shots were fired and Joe fell on
the floor,
He said, "In spite of all that's been I love my Ann the more."
His face was white as driven snow, his breath came gasping
low,
He said, "My soul is clean and to my Maker it must go."

Before he closed his dimming eye he said, "My work's not
done,"
And turning on his aching side he drew his faithful gun.
"You've done your mischief, stranger, but from life you've got
to part."
His finger pressed the trigger and he shot him through the
heart.

105

THE DARK GIRL DRESSED IN BLUE

'Twas on a Friday morning,
    The first day of August;
When of that day I ever think,
    My heart feels ready to bust!
I jumped into a Broadway stage,
    The Central Park going to,

On a seat by the right-hand side of the door,
  Sat a dark girl dressed in blue.

Now we hadn't gone very far,
  When the lady looked so strange;
The driver knocked down for his fare,
  Says she, "I have no change;
I've only a ten-dollar bill,
  O dear, what shall I do?"
Said I, "Allow me to pay," "O, thank you, sir,"
  Says the dark girl dressed in blue.

We chatted and talked as we onward walked,
  About one thing or the other;
She asked me, too (O wasn't it kind?)
  If I had a father or a mother.
Says I, "Yes, and a grandmother, too;
  But pray, miss, what are you?"
"O, I'm chief engineer in a milliner's shop,"
  Says the dark girl dressed in blue.

We walked about for an hour or two,
  Through the park, both near and far;
Then to a large hotel we went—
  I stepped up to the bar;
She slipped in my hand a ten-dollar bill,
  I said, "What are you going to do?"
"O, don't think it strange, I must have change."
  Said the dark girl dressed in blue.

We had some slight refreshments,
  And I handed out the bill;
The bar-keeper counted out the change,
  And the bill dropped in the till:

'Twas in currency and silver change;
  There was a three-cent piece or two;
So I rolled it up, and gave it to
  The dark girl dressed in blue.

She thanked me, and said, "I must away;
  Farewell, till next we meet;
For on urgent business I must go
  To the store in Hudson street."
She quickly glided from my sight,
  And soon was lost to view;
I turned to leave—when by my side
  Stood a tall man dressed blue!

This tall man said, "Excuse me, sir,
  I'm one of the 'special force';
That bill was bad—please come with me"—
  I had to go, of course.
Said I, "For a lady I obtained the change,"
  Says he, "Are you telling me true?
What's her name?" Says I, "I don't know,
  She was a dark girl dressed in blue."

My story they believed—thought I was deceived,
  But said I must hand back the cash;
I thought it was a sin, as I gave her the tin—
  Away went ten dollars smash!
So, all young men, take my advice,
  Be careful what you do,
When you make the acquaintance of ladies strange,
  Especially a dark girl dressed in blue.

106
SHE WAS POOR BUT SHE WAS HONEST

She was poor but she was honest,
   And her parents were the syme,
Till the county squire cyme courtin'
   And the poor girl lorst 'er nyme.

So she went aw'y to Lunnon,
   Just to 'ide 'er guilty shyme;
There she met an Army chaplain;
   Onst ag'in she lorst 'er nyme.

'Ear 'im as 'e jaws the Tommies,
   Warnin' of the flymes of 'ell,
With 'er 'ole 'eart she had trusted,
   But ag'in in sin she's fell.

So she settled down in Lunnon,
   Sinkin' deeper in 'er shyme,
Till she met a lybor leader,
   And ag'in she lorst 'er nyme.

See 'im in the 'ouse of Commons,
   Mykin' laws to put down crime,
While the poor girl that 'e's ruined
   Wanders on through mud and slime.

Then there cyme a bloated bishop;
   Marriage was the tyle 'e told,
There was no one else to tyke 'er,
   So she sold 'er soul for gold.

See 'er in 'er 'orse and carriage
   Drivin' d'ily through the park,
Though she's myde a wealthy marriage
   Still she 'ides a brykin' 'eart.

In their poor and 'umble dwelling,
   There 'er grievin' parents live,
Drinkin' champyne as she's sent 'em,
   But they never can forgive.

It's the syme the wide world over,
   It's the poor gets all the blyme,
While the rich gets all the clover.
   Ayn't it all a bloody shyme!

107

THE RICH COUNTRY GIRL AND THE WICKED CITY CHAP

It's all of a rich country girl that I know,
She plays the accordion and melodeon also,
With cheeks red as roses, and teeth like the snows,
She looks like an angel as a-milking she goes.

There was a young fellow, from the city he come,
He tried to entice her to leave her sweet home;
He gave her a locket, he gave her a ring,
And black Negro melodies he tried for to sing.

On one Sunday evening her father, says he,
"I want you to leave off this youth's company;

Of them counter-jumpers I pray you beware,
You will find them deceitful, I vow and declare."

Then the damsel she cried, and the damsel she wept,
She took to reading novels when she ought to have slept.
She left her melodeon and accordion also.
And a little while after she crazy did go.

MORAL

Now, all you pretty maidens that a lesson would learn,
Beware of these dandies, and their company spurn;
If you would not get raving, and crazy also,
When they come out to humbug, just tell them to go.

108

THE FROZEN MAID

Charlottie, the fair maid who gave her life for vanity (and
I hope this will be a lesson to you scantily clad damsels!) is
as old as the snows; as ageless as the icy winds that were her
winding shroud. She appears in the balladry of all peoples
who know the curse of cold. This version comes to us from—
of all places—the mountain regions of Georgia! It is impor-
tant to note that the maiden's name was Charlottie, not Char-
lotte. And I charge you to preserve the spelling and pronun-
ciation of "monoment" in the eighth stanza:

Charlottie liv'd on a mountain top in a bleak and lonely spot,
There were no other dwellings there except her father's cot.
And yet, on many a wintry night, young swains were gathered
    there;
Her father kept a social board and she was very fair.

On a New Year's Eve as the sun went down, far looked her
  wishful eye
Out from the frosty window pane as a merry sleigh dashed by.
At a village fifteen miles away was to be a ball that night,
And though the air was piercing cold her heart was warm
  and light.

How brightly gleamed her laughing eye, as a well known
  voice she heard;
And dashing up to the cottage door her lover's sleigh appeared.
"Oh, daughter dear," her mother cried, "This blanket round
  you fold,
Tonight is a dreadful one, you'll get your death of cold."

"Oh, nay, oh nay!" Charlottie cried, as she laughed like a
  gypsy queen,
"To ride in blankets muffled up I never would be seen;
My silken cloak is quite enough, you know 'tis lined throughout,
And there's my silken scarf to twine my head and neck
  about."

Her bonnet and her gloves were on, she leaped into the
  sleigh,
And swiftly they sped down the mountain side and o'er the
  hills away.
With muffled beat so silently five miles at length were passed,
When Charles with a few and shivering words the silence
  broke at last.

"Such a dreadful night, I never saw, the reins I scarce can
  hold,"
Charlottie faintly then replied, "I am exceeding cold."

He cracked his whip, he urged his steed much faster than
    before;
And thus five other weary miles in silence were passed o'er.

Said Charles: "How fast the shivering ice is gathering on my
    brow,"
And Charlott' then more faintly cried, "I'm growing warmer
    now."
Thus on they rode through frosty air and the glittering cold
    starlight,
Until at last the village lamps and the ballroom came in sight.

They reached the door and Charles sprang out, he reached his
    hand to her,
"Why set you there like a monoment that has no power to
    stir?"
He called her once, he called her twice, she answered not a
    word;
He asked her for her hands again, but still she never stirred.

He took her hand in his,—'twas cold and hard as any stone;
He tore the mantle from her face, the cold stars o'er it shone.
Then quickly to the lighted hall her lifeless form he bore;
Charlottie's eyes had closed for aye, her voice was heard no
    more.

And there he sat down by her side, while bitter tears did flow
And cried, "My own, my charming bride, 'tis you may never
    know."
He twined his arms around her neck, he kissed her marble
    brow;
His thoughts flew back to where she said, "I'm growing
    warmer now."

109

THE ORPHAN GIRL,

or

NO BREAD FOR THE POOR

This is the pattern song upon which Ed Marks and his compatriots of the Gilded Era based innumerable heart-rending variations. It traces back, strangely enough, to the Appalachians, where rich men on velvet couches are a rarity, and everyone is quite unconcernedly "pore." Speculating on an earlier origin, we may well assume that the substance of the ballad was, like many another mountain song, imported from England:

"No home, no home," cried an orphan girl
  At the door of a princely hall,
As she trembling stood on the polished steps
  And leaned on the marble wall.

Her clothes were torn and her head was bare
  And she tried to cover her feet
With her dress that was tattered and covered with snow,
  Yes, covered with snow and sleet.

Her dress was thin and her feet were bare
  And the snow had covered her head.
"Oh, give me a home," she feebly cried,
  "A home and a piece of bread."

"My father, alas, I never knew."
  Tears dimmed the eyes so bright.
"My mother sleeps in a new-made grave,
  'Tis an orphan that begs to-night."

"I must freeze," she cried as she sank on the steps
  And strove to cover her feet
With her ragged garments covered with snow,
  Yes, covered with snow and sleet.

The rich man lay on his velvet couch
  And dreamed of his silver and gold
While the orphan girl in her bed of snow
  Was murmuring, "So cold, so cold."

The night was dark and the snow fell fast
  As the rich man closed his door,
And his proud lips curled with scorn as he said,
  "No bread, no room, for the poor."

The morning dawned but the orphan girl
  Still lay at the rich man's door
And her soul had fled to that home above
  Where there's bread and room for the poor.

110

POPULAR BALLAD: "NEVER FORGET YOUR PARENTS"

The mock-ballad was an inevitable development of our
teeming times. So rich a field for the parodists could not well
be left untilled. This example, from the typewriter of the il-
lustrious "F. P. A." well serves our point:

> A young man once was sitting
>   Within a swell café,
> The music it was playing sweet—
>   The people was quite gay.

But he alone was silent,
  A tear was in his eye—
A waitress she stepped up to him, and
  Asked him gently why.

      (Change to Minor)

He turned to her in sorrow and
  At first he spoke no word,
But soon he spoke unto her, for
  She was an honest girl.
He rose up from the table
  In that elegant café,
And in a voice replete with tears
  To her he then did say:

      (Chorus)

Never forget your father,
  Think all he done for you;
A mother is a boy's best friend,
  So loving, kind, and true,
If it were not for them, I'm sure
  I might be quite forlorn;
And if your parents had not have lived
  You would not have been born.

A hush fell on the laughing throng,
  It made them feel quite bad,
For most of them was people, and
  Some parents they had had.
Both men and ladies did shed tears,
  The music it did cease,
For all knew he had spoke the truth
  By looking at his face.

(Change to Minor)

The waitress she wept bitterly
　And others was in tears
It made them think of the old home
　They had not saw in years.
And while their hearts was heavy and
　Their eyes they was quite red,
This brave and honest boy again
　To them these words he said:

(Chorus)

Never forget your father,
　Think all he done for you;
A mother is a boy's best friend,
　So loving, kind, and true,
If it were not for them, I'm sure
　I might be quite forlorn;
And if your parents had not have lived
　You would not have been born.
　　　　　　—*Franklin P. Adams.*

111

JOHN HENRY

John Henry is the John Bunyan of the bayous, the tireless titan of the Negro race. While, in this version, John Henry meets his doom, we need not be dismayed. He is resurrected with feline fecundity in the imagination of the black man, rising always to new and greater exploits. Once when Roark Bradford, John Henry's current Boswell, asked a Negro narrator how the prodigious black man could be in two places simultaneously, his informant blandly replied, "Jawn Henry he is a man what gits about."

John Henry tol' his cap'n
Dat a man wuz a natural man,
An' befo' he'd let dat steam drill run him down
He'd fall dead wid a hammer in his han',
He'd fall dead wid a hammer in his han'!

Cap'n he sez to John Henry:
"Gonna bring me a steam drill 'round;
Take that steel drill out on the job,
Gonna whop that steel on down,
Gonna whop that steel on down."

John Henry sez to his cap'n:
"Send me a twelve-poun' hammer aroun',
A twelve-poun' hammer wid a fo'-foot handle.
An' I beat yo' steam drill down,
An' I beat yo' steam drill down."

John Henry sez to his shaker:
"Niggah, why don' yo' sing?
I'm throwin' twelve poun' from my hips on down,
Jes' lissen to de col' steel ring,
Jes' lissen to do col' steel ring!"

John Henry went down de railroad
Wid a twelve-poun' hammer by his side,
He walked down de track but he didn' come back,
'Cause he laid down his hammer an' he died,
'Cause he laid down his hammer an' he died.

John Henry hammered in de mountains,
De mountains wuz so high.
De las' words I heard de pore boy say:

"Gimme a cool drink o' watah fo' I die,
Gimme a cool drink o' watah fo' I die!"

John Henry had a little baby,
Hel' him in de palm of his han'.
De las' words I heard de pore boy say:
"Son, yo're gonna be a steel-drivin' man,
Son, yo're gonna be a steel-drivin' man!"

John Henry had a 'ooman,
De dress she wo' wuz blue.
De las' words I heard de pore gal say:
"John Henry, I ben true to yo',
John Henry, I ben true to yo'."

John Henry had a li'l 'ooman,
De dress she wo' wuz brown.
De las' words I heard de pore gal say:
"I'm goin' w'eah mah man went down,
I'm goin' w'eah mah man went down!"

John Henry had anothah 'ooman,
De dress she wo' wuz red.
De las' words I heard de pore gal say:
"I'm goin' w'eah mah man drapt daid,
I'm goin' w'eah mah man drapt daid!"

John Henry had a li'l 'ooman,
Her name wuz Polly Ann.
On de day John Henry he drap daid
Polly Ann hammered steel like a man,
Polly Ann hammered steel like a man.

W'eah did yo' git dat dress!
W'eah did you git dose shoes so fine?
Got dat dress f'm off a railroad man,
An' shoes f'm a driver in a mine,
An' shoes f'm a driver in a mine.

112

FIRE

Amongst the modern ballad-writers, the Negro minne-singer, Langston Hughes has won renown for the simple sin-cerity of his songs of humble folk. A good example is this burning ballad of the imaginative black man:

Fire,
Fire, Lord!
Fire gonna burn ma soul!

I ain't been good,
I ain't been clean—
I been stinkin', low-down, mean.

Fire,
Fire, Lord!
Fire gonna burn ma soul!

Tell me, brother,
Do you believe
If you wanta go to heaben
Got to moan an' grieve?

Fire,
Fire, Lord!
Fire gonna burn ma soul!

I been stealin',
Been tellin' lies;
Had more women
Than Pharaoh had wives.

Fire,
Fire, Lord!
Fire gonna burn ma soul!
I means Fire, Lord!
Fire gonna burn ma soul.
                    —*Langston Hughes.*

VII

THE STAG IN MERRY MOOD

It is enough that you and I,
  Whatever be our girth,
Shake a fist at fret and gloom
  And gird the day with mirth.

—*Father Jerome.*

THE POST THAT FITTED

Ere the steamer bore him Eastward, Sleary was engaged to
  marry
An attractive girl at Tunbridge, whom he called "my little
  Carrie."
Sleary's pay was very modest; Sleary was the other way.
Who can cook a two-plate dinner on eight poor rupees a
  day?

Long he pondered o'er the question in his scantly furnished
  quarters—
Then proposed to Minnie Boffkin, eldest of Judge Boffkin's
  daughters.
Certainly an impecunious Subaltern was not a catch,
But the Boffkins knew that Minnie mightn't make another
  match.

So they recognised the business and, to feed and clothe the
  bride,
Got him made a Something Something somewhere on the
  Bombay side.
Anyhow, the billet carried pay enough for him to marry—
As the artless Sleary put it:—"Just the thing for me and
  Carrie."

Did he, therefore, jilt Miss Boffkin—impulse of a baser mind?
No! He started epileptic fits of an appalling kind.
(Of his *modus operandi* only this much I could gather:—
"Pear's shaving sticks will give you little taste and lots of
  lather.")

Frequently in public places his affliction used to smite
Sleary with distressing vigour—always in the Boffkins' sight.
Ere a week was over Minnie weepingly returned his ring,
Told him his "unhappy weakness" stopped all thought of
    "marrying."

Sleary bore the information with a chastened holy joy,—
Epileptic fits don't matter in Political employ,—
Wired three short words to Carrie—took his ticket, packed
    his kit—
Bade farewell to Minnie Boffkin in one last, long, lingering
    fit.

Four weeks later, Carrie Sleary read—and laughed until she
    wept—
Mrs. Boffkin's warning letter on the "wretched epilept." . . .
Year by year, in pious patience, vengeful Mrs. Boffkin sits
Waiting for the Sleary babies to develop Sleary's fits.

                        —*Rudyard Kipling.*

114

A DIRGE

Concerning The Late Lamented King Of The Cannibal Islands

And so our royal relative is dead!
   And so he rests from gustatory labors!
The white man was his choice, but when he fed
   He'd sometimes entertain his tawny neighbors.
He worshipped, as he said, his "Fe-fo-fum,"
The goddess of the epigastrium.

And missionaries graved his festive board,
  Solemn and succulent, in twos and dozens,
And smoked before their hospitable lord,
  Welcome as if they'd been his second cousins.
When cold, he warmed them as he would his kin—
They came as strangers, and he took them in.

And generous!—oh, wasn't he? I have known him
  Exhibit a celestial amiability:—
He'd eat an enemy, and then would own him
  Of flavor excellent, despite hostility.
The cruelest captain of the Turkish navy
He buried in an honorable grav—y.

He had a hundred wives. To make things pleasant
  They found it quite judicious to adore him;—
And when he dined, the nymphs were always present—
  Sometimes beside him and sometimes—before him.
When he was tired of one, he called her "sweet,"
And told her she was "good enough to eat."

He was a man of taste—and justice, too;
  He opened his mouth for e'en the humblest sinner,
And three weeks stall-fed an emaciate Jew
  Before they brought him to the royal dinner.
With preacher-men he shared his board and wallet
And let them nightly occupy his palate!

We grow like what we eat. Bad food depresses;
  Good food exalts us like an inspiration,
And missionary on the *menu* blesses
  And elevates the Feejee population.

A people who for years, saints, bairs, and women ate
Must soon their vilest qualities eliminate.

But the deceased could never hold a candle
  To those prim, pale-faced people of propriety
Who gloat o'er gossip and get fat on scandal—
  The cannibals of civilized society;
They drink the blood of brothers with their rations,
And crunch the bones of living reputations.

They kill the soul; he only claimed the dwelling.
  They take the sharpened scalpel of surmises
And cleave the sinews when the heart is swelling,
  And slaughter Fame and Honor for their prizes.
They make the spirit in the body quiver;
They quench the Light! He only took the—Liver!

I've known some hardened customers, I wot,
  A few tough fellows—pagans beyond question—
I wish had got into his dinner-pot;
  Although I'm certain they'd defy digestion,
And break his jaw, and ruin his esophagus,
Were he the chief of beings anthropophagous!

How fond he was of children! To his breast
  The tenderest nurslings gained a free admission.
Rank he despised, nor, if they came well dressed,
  Cared if they were plebeian or patrician.
Shade of Leigh Hunt! Oh, guide this laggard pen
To write of one who loved his fellow men!
                              —*William Augustus Croffut.*

115

ETIQUETTE

The *Ballyshannon* foundered off the coast of Cariboo,
And down in fathoms many went the captain and the crew;
Down went the owners—greedy men whom hope of gain
    allured:
Oh, dry the starting tear, for they were heavily insured.

Besides the captain and the mate, the owners and the crew,
The passengers were also drowned excepting only two:
Young Peter Gray, who tasted teas for Baker, Croop, and
    Co.,
And Somers, who from Eastern shores imported indigo.

These passengers, by reason of their clinging to a mast,
Upon a desert island were eventually cast.
They hunted for their meals, as Alexander Selkirk used,
But they couldn't chat together—they had not been intro-
    duced.

For Peter Gray, and Somers, too, though certainly in trade,
Were properly particular about the friends they made;
And somehow thus they settled it, without a word of
    mouth,
That Gray should take the northern half, while Somers took
    the south.

On Peter's portion oysters grew—a delicacy rare,
But oysters were a delicacy Peter couldn't bear.
On Somer's side was turtle, on the shingle lying thick,
Which Somers couldn't eat, because it always made him
    sick.

Gray gnashed his teeth with envy as he saw a mighty store
Of turtle unmolested on his fellow-creature's shore.
The oysters at his feet aside impatiently he shoved,
For turtle and his mother were the only things he loved.

And Somers sighed in sorrow as he settled in the south,
For the thought of Peter's oysters brought the water to his
    mouth.
He longed to lay him down upon the shelly bed, and stuff:
He had often eaten oysters, but had never had enough.

How they wished an introduction to each other they had
    had
When on board the *Ballyshannon!* And it drove them
    nearly mad
To think how very friendly with each other they might get,
If it wasn't for the arbitrary rule of etiquette!

One day, when out a-hunting for the *mus ridiculus,*
Gray overheard his fellow-man soliloquising thus:
"I wonder how the playmates of my youth are getting on,
M'Connell, S. B. Walters, Paddy Byles, and Robinson?"

These simple words made Peter as delighted as could be;
Old chummies at the Charterhouse were Robinson and he.
He walked straight up to Somers, then he turned extremely
    red,
Hesitated, hummed and hawed a bit, then cleared his
    throat, and said:

"I beg your pardon—pray forgive me if I seem too bold,
But you have breathed a name I knew familiarly of old.
You spoke aloud of Robinson—I happened to be by.
You know him?" "Yes, extremely well." "Allow me, so do I."

It was enough: they felt they could more pleasantly get on,
For (ah, the magic of the fact!) they each knew Robinson!
And Mr. Somers' turtle was at Peter's service quite,
And Mr. Somers punished Peter's oyster-beds all night.

They soon became like brothers from community of
    wrongs;
They wrote each other little odes and sang each other
    songs;
They told each other anecdotes disparaging their wives;
On several occasions, too, they saved each other's lives.

They felt quite melancholy when they parted for the night,
And got up in the morning soon as ever it was light;
Each other's pleasant company they reckoned so upon,
And all because it happened that they both knew Robinson!

They lived for many years on that inhospitable shore,
And day by day they learned to love each other more and
    more.
At last, to their astonishment, on getting up one day,
They saw a frigate anchored in the offing of the bay.

To Peter an idea occurred. "Suppose we cross the main?
So good an opportunity may not be found again."
And Somers thought a minute, then ejaculated, "Don!
I wonder how my business in the City's getting on?"

"But stay," said Mr. Peter; "when in England, as you know,
I earned a living tasting teas for Baker, Croop, and Co.,
I may be superseded—my employers think me dead!"
"Then come with me," said Somers, "and taste indigo in-
    stead."

But all their plans were scattered in a moment when they
found
The vessel was a convict ship from Portland outward
bound;
When a boat came off to fetch them, though they felt it
very kind,
To go on board they firmly but respectfully declined.

As both the happy settlers roared with laughter at the joke,
They recognized a gentlemanly fellow pulling stroke:
'Twas Robinson—a convict, in an unbecoming frock!
Condemned to seven years for misappropriating stock!!!

They laughed no more, for Somers thought he had been
rather rash
In knowing one whose friend had misappropriated cash;
And Peter thought a foolish tack he must have gone upon
In making the acquaintance of a friend of Robinson.

At first they didn't quarrel very openly, I've heard;
They nodded when they met, and now and then exchanged
a word:
The word grew rare, and rarer still the nodding of the
head.
And when they meet each other now, they cut each other
dead.

To allocate the island they agreed by word of mouth,
And Peter takes the north again, and Somers takes the
south;
And Peter has the oysters, which he hates in layers thick,
And Somers has the turtle—turtle always makes him sick.

—*W. S. Gilbert.*

116

A GREAT FIGHT

"There was a man in Arkansaw
  As let his passions rise,
And not unfrequently picked out
  Some other varmint's eyes.

"His name was Tuscaloosa Sam
  And often he would say,
'There's not a cuss in Arkansaw
  I can't whip any day.'

"One morn, a stranger passin' by,
  Heard Sammy talkin' so,
And down he scrambled from his hoss,
  And off his coat did go.

"He sorter kinder shut one eye,
  And spit into his hand,
And put his ugly head one side,
  And twitched his trousers' band.

" 'My boy,' says he, 'it's my belief,
  Whomever you may be,
That I kin make you screech, and smell
  Pertiklor agony.'

" 'I'm thar,' said Tuscaloosa Sam,
  And chucked his hat away;
'I'm thar,' says he, and buttoned up
  As far as buttons may.

"He thundered on the stranger's mug,
  The stranger pounded he;
And oh! the way them critters fit
  Was beautiful to see.

"They clinched like two rampageous bears,
  And then went down a bit;
They swore a stream of six-inch oaths
  And fit, and fit, and fit.

"When Sam would try to work away,
  And on his pegs to git,
The stranger'd pull him back; and so,
  They fit, and fit, and fit!

"Then like a pair of lobsters, both
  Upon the ground were knit,
And yet the varmints used their teeth,
  And fit, and fit, and fit!!

"The sun of noon was high above,
  And hot enough to split,
But only riled the fellers more,
  That fit, and fit, and fit!!!

"The stranger snapped at Sammy's nose,
  And shortened it a bit;
And then they both swore awful hard,
  And fit, and fit, and fit!!!!

"The mud it flew, the sky grew dark,
  And all the litenins lit;
But still them critters rolled about,
  And fit, and fit, and fit!!!!!

"First Sam on top, then t'other chap;
　When one would make a hit,
The other'd smell the grass; and so
　They fit, and fit, and fit!!!!!!

"The night came on, the stars shone out
　As bright as wimmen's wit;
And still them fellers swore and gouged,
　And fit, and fit, and fit!!!!!!!

"The neighbours heard the noise they made,
　And thought an earthquake lit;
Yet all the while 'twas him and Sam
　As fit and fit, and fit!!!!!!!!

"For miles around the noise was heard;
　Folks couldn't sleep a bit,
Because them two rantankerous chaps
　Still fit, and fit, and fit!!!!!!!!!

"But jist at cock-crow, suddenly,
　There came an awful pause,
And I and my old man run out
　To ascertain the cause.

"The sun was rising in the yeast
　And lit the hull concern;
But not a sign of either chap
　Was found at any turn.

"Yet, in the region where they fit,
　We found, to our surprise,
One pint of buttons, two big knives,
　Some whiskers, and four eyes!"
　　　　　　　—*Robert Henry Newell.*

117

PLAIN LANGUAGE FROM TRUTHFUL JAMES

Table Mountain, 1870

Which I wish to remark—
  And my language is plain—
That for ways that are dark,
  And for tricks that are vain,
The heathen Chinee is peculiar,
  Which the same I would rise to explain.

Ah Sin was his name;
  And I will not deny
In regard to the same
  What that name might imply;
But his smile it was pensive and childlike,
  As I frequent remarked to Bill Nye.

It was August the third;
  And quite soft was the skies:
Which it might be inferred
  That Ah Sin was likewise;
Yet he played it that day upon William
  And me in a way I despise.

Which we had a small game,
  And Ah Sin took a hand.
It was Euchre. The same
  He did not understand;
But he smiled as he sat by the table,
  With a smile that was childlike and bland.

Yet the cards they were stocked
  In a way that I grieve,
And my feelings were shocked

At the state of Nye's sleeve:
Which was stuffed full of aces and bowers,
    And the same with intent to deceive.

But the hands that were played
    By that heathen Chinee,
And the points that he made,
    Were quite frightful to see—
Till at last he put down a right bower,
    Which the same Nye had dealt unto me.

Then I looked up at Nye,
    And he gazed upon me;
And he rose with a sigh,
    And said, "Can this be?
We are ruined by Chinese cheap labour—"
    And he went for that heathen Chinee.

In the scene that ensued
    I did not take a hand;
But the floor it was strewed
    Like the leaves on the strand
With the cards that Ah Sin had been hiding,
    In the game "he did not understand."

In his sleeves, which were long,
    He had twenty-four packs—
Which was coming it strong,
    Yet I state but the facts;
And we found on his nails, which were taper,
    What is frequent in tapers—that's wax.

Which is why I remark,
    And my language is plain,
That for ways that are dark,
    And for tricks that are vain,

The heathen Chinee is peculiar—
Which the same I am free to maintain.

—*Bret Harte.*

118

FINNIGIN TO FLANNIGAN

Superintendent wuz Flannigan;
Boss av the siction wuz Finnigin;
Whiniver the kyars got offen the thrack,
An' muddled up things t' th' divil an' back,
Finnigin writ it to Flannigan,
Afther the wrick wuz all on ag'in;
    That is, this Finnigin
    Repoorted to Flannigan.

Whin Finnigin furst writ to Flannigan,
He writed tin pages—did Finnigin,
An' he tould jist how the smash occurred;
Full minny a tajus, blunderin' wurrd
Did Finnigin write to Flannigan
Afther the cars had gone on ag'in.
    That wuz how Finnigin
    Repoorted to Flannigan.

Now Flannigan knowed more than Finnigin—
He'd more idjucation, had Flannigan;
An' it wore'm clane an' complately out
To tell what Finnigin writ about
In his writin' to Muster Flannigan.
So he writed back to Finnigin:
    "Don't do sich a sin ag'in;
    Make 'em brief, Finnigin!"

Whin Finnigin got this from Flannigan,
He blushed rosy rid, did Finnigin;
An' he said: "I'll gamble a whole month's pa-ay
That it will be minny an' minny a da-ay
Befoore Sup'rintindint—that's Flannigan—
Gits a whack at this very same sin ag'in.
　From Finnigin to Flannigan
　Repoorts won't be long ag'in."

Wan da-ay, on the siction av Finnigin,
On the road sup'rintinded by Flannigan,
A rail give way on a bit av a curve,
An' some kyars went off as they made the swerve.
"There's nobody hurted," sez Finnigin,
"But repoorts must be made to Flannigan."
　An' he winked at McGorrigan,
　As married a Finnigin.

He wuz shantyin' thin, wuz Finnigin,
As minny a railroader's been ag'in,
An' the shmoky ol' lamp wuz burnin' bright
In Finnigin's shanty all that night—
Bilin' down his repoort, was Finnigin!
An' he writed this here: "Muster Flannigan:
　Off ag'in, on ag'in,
　Gon ag'in—Finnigin."
　　　　　　　　　—*Strickland Gillilan.*

119

HEM AND HAW

Hem and Haw were the sons of sin,
Created to shally and shirk;

Hem lay 'round and Haw looked on
While God did all the work.

Hem was foggy, and Haw was a prig,
For both had the dull, dull mind;
And whenever they found a thing to do,
They yammered and went it blind.

Hem was the father of bigots and bores;
As the sands of the sea were they.
And Haw was the father of all the tribe
Who criticize today.

But God was an artist from the first,
And knew what he was about;
While over his shoulder sneered these two,
And advised him to rub it out.

They prophesied ruin ere man was made;
"Such folly must surely fail!"
And when he was done, "Do you think, my Lord,
He's better without a tail?"

And still in the honest working world,
With posture and hint and smirk,
These sons of the devil are standing by
While man does all the work.

They balk endeavor and baffle reform,
In the sacred name of law;
And over the quavering voice of Hem
Is the droning voice of Haw.

—Bliss Carman.

120

THE ROMANCE OF REX

(A Tale of a Pedigreed Piddlin' Pup in Ten Piddles and a Puddle)

Once upon a time, following persistent prodding from associates, your editor included this *vulgarité* in a small collection of salty verse. So instant and insistent was the clamour for additional copies, that we felt an obligation to retain the selection through numerous subsequent editions. The story of Rex has been widely quoted—usually without due credit. It was written, many years ago, by Jo Anderson who is now a retired druggist, living at Chattanooga, Tennessee. We include it in this anthology at the specific request of many readers who seek a more enduring record of their favorite poem:

Piddle No. 1

A Farmer's dog came into town,
    His christian name was Rex.
A noble pedigree had he;
    Unusual was his text.
And as he trotted down the street
    'Twas beautiful to see
His work on every corner—
    His work on every tree.

Piddle No. 2

He watered every gateway too,
    And never missed a post,
For piddling was his specialty
    And piddling was his boast.
The City Curs looked on amazed,
    With deep and jealous rage

To see a simple country dog
   The piddler of the age.

Piddle No. 3

Then all the dogs from everywhere
   Were summoned with a yell,
To sniff the country stranger o'er
   And judge him by the smell.
Some thought that he a king might be;
   Beneath his tail a rose.
So every dog drew near to him
   And sniffed it up his nose.

Piddle No. 4

They smelled him over one by one
   They smelled him two by two
And noble Rex, in high disdain
   Stood still till they were through.
Then, just to show the whole shebang
   He didn't give a damn,
He trotted in a grocery store
   And piddled on a ham.

Piddle No. 5

He piddled on a mackerel keg—
   He piddled on the floor,
And when the grocer kicked him out,
   He piddled through the door.
Behind him all the city dogs
   Lined up with instinct true
To start a piddling carnival
   And see the stranger through.

Piddle No. 6

They showed him every piddling post
  They had in all the town,
And started in with many a wink
  To pee the stranger down.
They sent for champion piddlers
  Who were always on the go,
Who sometimes did a piddling stunt
  Or gave a piddle show.

Piddle No. 7

They sprung these on him suddenly,
  When midway of the town;
Rex only smiled and polished off
  The ablest, white or brown.
For Rex was with them every trick
  With vigor and with vim.
A thousand piddles, more or less,
  Were all the same to him.

Piddle No. 8

So he was wetting merrily
  With hind leg kicking high,
When most were hoisting legs in bluff
  And piddling mighty dry.
On and on, Rex sought new grounds
  By piles and scraps and rust,
'Til every city dog went dry
  And piddled only dust.

Piddle No. 9

But on and on went noble Rex
  As wet as any rill,

And all the champion city pups
 Were pee'd to a standstill.
Then Rex did free-hand piddling,
 With fancy flirts and flits
Like "double-dip" and "gimlet twist"
 And all those latest hits.

Piddle No. 10

And all the time this country dog
 Did never wink or grin,
But piddled blithely out of town
 As he had piddled in.

The Puddle

The city dogs conventions held
 To ask, "What did defeat us?"
But no one ever put them wise
 That Rex had diabetes.

—*Jo Anderson.*

121

SOME LITTLE BUG

In these days of indigestion
It is oftentimes a question
 As to what to eat and what to leave alone;
For each microbe and bacillus
Has a different way to kill us,
 And in time they always claim us for their own.
There are germs of every kind
In any food that you can find

In the market or upon the bill of fare.
Drinking water's just as risky
As the so-called deadly whiskey,
   And it's often a mistake to breathe the air.

Some little bug is going to find you some day,
Some little bug will creep behind you some day,
   Then he'll send for his bug friends
   And all your earthly trouble ends;
Some little bug is going to find you some day.

The inviting green cucumber
Gets most everybody's number,
   While the green corn has a system of its own;
Though a radish seems nutritious
Its behaviour is quite vicious,
   And a doctor will be coming to your home.
Eating lobster cooked or plain
Is only flirting with ptomaine,
   While an oyster sometimes has a lot to say,
But the clams we eat in chowder
Make the angels chant the louder,
   For they know that we'll be with them right
     away.

Take a slice of nice fried onion
And you're fit for Dr. Munyon,
   Apple dumplings kill you quicker than a train.
Chew a cheesy midnight "rabbit"
And a grave you'll soon inhabit—
   Ah, to eat at all is such a foolish game.
Eating huckleberry pie
Is a pleasing way to die,

While sauerkraut brings on softening of the
    brain.
When you eat banana fritters
Every undertaker titters,
    And the casket makers nearly go insane.

Some little bug is going to find you some day,
Some little bug will creep behind you some day,
    With a nervous little quiver
    He'll give cirrhosis of the liver;
Some little bug is going to find you some day.

When cold storage vaults I visit
I can only say what is it
    Makes poor mortals fill their systems with such
        stuff?
Now, for breakfast, prunes are dandy
If a stomach pump is handy
    And your doctor can be found quite soon
        enough.
Eat a plate of fine pigs' knuckles
And the headstone cutter chuckles,
    While the grave digger makes a note upon his
        cuff.
Eat that lovely red bologna
And you'll wear a wooden kimona,
    As your relatives start scrappin' 'bout your stuff.

Some little bug is going to find you some day,
Some little bug will creep behind you some day,
    Eating juicy sliced pineapple
    Makes the sexton dust the chapel;
Some little bug is going to find you some day.

All those crazy foods they mix
Will float us 'cross the River Styx,
   Or they'll start us climbing up the milky way.
And the meals we eat in courses
Mean a hearse and two black horses
   So before a meal some always pray.
Luscious grapes breed 'pendicitis,
And the juice leads to gastritis,
   So there's only death to greet us either way;
And fried liver's nice, but, mind you,
Friends will soon ride slow behind you
   And the papers then will have nice things to
     say.

Some little bug is going to find you some day,
Some little bug will creep behind you some day
   Eat some sauce, they call it chili,
   On your breast they'll place a lily;
Some little bug is going to find you some day.
                —*Roy Atwell.*

122

BEAU NIGHT

Can't you recall, how in days of yore,
At three o'clock or maybe four,
Or five, of a Sunday afternoon,
You'd a little rather, or just as soon,
Hitch your "rig" to the picket fence,
And loaded down with confidence,

Enter the house to play your part
In winnin' a lady's guileless heart,
With a package of Sen Sens, and cut-away
    clothes,
A big four-in-hand, and striped hose,
We've gone to the parlors with faces alight,
For Sunday was Sunday and always beau night.

And the poor old horse would stand and stand,
While you were holdin' the lady's hand.
Poor old horse, but wonderful hand!
Wonderful! wonderful!! wonderful hand! ! !
And the poor old horse would paw the ground,
While you were slippin' your arm around
The back of the sofa, carelessly there,
And tryin' to act like you didn't know where,
In the course of time, saucer and cup,
That arm of yours would be finishin' up.
Oh, we've been there, and there wasn't much
    light,
For Sunday was Sunday and always beau night.

Your horse would whinny—softly cursin' these
    trips—
But he didn't know you were pressin' her lips,
And he had no way to even guess
That she was sayin' that wonderful "Yes."
But he surely did know you were tryin' your hand
At stretchin' the night like a rubber band
Into two or three times its normal length,
And wasting his patience as well as his strength.
Well, those days are gone, and the "rig" that was
    real
Has long been replaced by the automobile.

Their outfits now are speedy and light,
But Sunday's still Sunday and always beau night.
—*Barton Rees Pogue.*

123

I WISH I COULD LEARN TO LAUGH AT MYSELF

I wish I could learn to laugh at myself
   Somehow have the wisdom to see
That the very best joke in all of the world
   Is the fellow that I call me.
I know I'm not Utopia's king,
   I allow I'm a laughable joint,
But in spite of the fact that I know I'm a joke
   I never have quite seen the point.

I wish I could learn to laugh at myself,
   To roar at my funny ears,
Fall in a fit at the sight of my legs
   And the way my big nose steers;
If I only could laugh, like you always do,
   At the whimsical things I have done,
I'd start in and laugh out the days of old age
   And surely have lots of fun.

I wish I could learn to laugh at myself,
   'Twould save me a lot of conceit,
And show me that out of earth's harvest of souls
   I'm not quite the choice of the wheat.
'Twould save me from being a Pharisee,

From looking on life so sour,
And seriously thinking to save mankind
   By the strength of my own great power.

O, I wish I could learn to laugh at myself,
   For it seems that a good funny streak
Would help me rejoice in the strength of the
   strong,
   And lend a kind hand to the weak.
'Twould level my airs and pull up my gloom,
   And make me a man loved of men,
So here's to the hope that I start in today
   And never stop laughing again.
               —*Barton Rees Pogue.*

124

LADIES FIRST

"Oh, do you mind," the lady said,
"If I step in and go ahead?
I hope that you will pardon me,
But I am in a rush, you see.
I'm going out today to dine.
Would you give me your place in line?"
And so I smile a gracious smile,
And meekly bow and lift my tile.
I do not mind just doing this,
It helps to add to human bliss;
But when the females all combine
To come and take my place in line,
My temper seems to soar and burst.
Who wrote that saying, "Ladies First"?
               —*George F. Goodman.*

125

All the world's a club,
And all the girls and women merely joiners:
They have their fancies and their favorites;
And one woman in her time joins many clubs,
Throughout her seven stages. At first, she's timid;
Draws back and nestles in her quiet home;
And then, the charming young girl, with her note-
    book,
And sunny, beaming face, walking, like Eve,
Unwittingly to doom. And then, the zealot;
Talking like magpie, with a joyful ballot
Made for her chairman's glory. Then, a speaker,
Full of strange words, and flurried like the club;
Zealous in instinct, rapid and sure in method,
Seeking the bubble reputation
Even in the enemy's glare. And then, the matron,
Her fair, round figure, cloth outside and silk lin'd,
Full of witty quips and modern instances,
And thus she reads her paper. The sixth age leads
Into the gray and silvered devotee,
With lorgnette in hand, and bag at side;
Her youthful gown well covered, a world too small
For her decorations, and her many badges
Shining in all their gorgeous array, show
Allegiance to her clubs. Last scene of all
That ends this strange, eventful history,
Is daily attendance at each society;
Sans aim, sans love, sans home, sans everything.
                    —*A Parody, by Nellie Howes.*

126

I ENVY MY NEIGHBOR'S HOUSE

Dusty beam and blackened wall,
Wormy wood: a dusky hall,

Mellowed: a long lantern hung,
Swinging: cracked walls: cobwebs strung

In festoons: an ancient lamp,
Grease-marked: everywhere the stamp

Of the ages: furniture,
Hewn and rusty, with the lure

Of a dozen centuries:
Oh, I love things old as these!

How I wish I could afford
Such a home: But, oh, my lord!

It takes a minted heap of gold
To make a new house look so old!
—*Wilfred J. Funk.*

127

MERRY-MAKING PARSON

A teacher in a Sunday School, to give her class delight,
Had all her little students at a party Christmas night.
The parson of the church had heard the children would
    convene
And thought it would be jolly to look in upon the scene;

And so he donned his coat and hat and happily set out
To see his little flock at play—a pastoral "good scout."
He rang the doorbell and, admitted to the entrance hall,
He told the servant: "Don't announce me; I'll surprise
'em all."
With coat and hat removed, the parson quietly drew near
The spacious parlors from whence came the buzz of voices
clear.
Then down on hands and knees he went, and bounded in
that way,
Emitting funny noises something like a horse's neigh.
A deadly silence followed; he glanced upward from the
floor,
And saw a formal dinner group; his kiddies were next
door!

128

THE BLASÉ MAN

This world is but a bubble, doncherknow;
Its full of twials and twouble, doncherknow
    You come to earth to cwy,
    You grow oldah and you sigh—
Oldah still and then—you die, doncherknow.

And its all a howid mix, doncherknow;
Bussiness, love and politics, doncherknow;
    Fashions, follies, cliques and sets,
    Clubs and pawties, sighs, wegwets,
Struggle, stwife,—and cigawettes doncherknow.

Bussiness! Ah, thats twade doncherknow;
Something lost or something made doncherknow;

You stwuggle and you mope,
And you hang your highest hope
On perhaps the pwice of—soap doncherknow.

Fashion! Ah, thats dwess doncherknow;
The cause of much distwess, doncherknow;
   To determine what to weah,
   When to go and likewise whea,
And how to part your haih, doncherknow.

Politics! Just a lawk doncherknow;
Just a nightmare in the dawk doncherknow;
   You perspire day and night,
   And after all the fight,
Why—perhaps the wrong man's wight, doncherknow.

Love! Ah yes! You meet a girl doncherknow;
And you get in such a whirl doncherknow;
   You get down upon the floah
   To adoah and imploah,
And its all a howwid boah, doncherknow.

For there's weally nothing in it, doncherknow;
For you live for just a minute, doncherknow;
   When you've eaten, read and felt,
   Heard and seen and said and smelt,
Why—All the cawds are dealt, doncherknow.

You've one consciousness, that's all doncherknow;
One stomach and thats small doncherknow;
   You can only weah one tie,
   And one eyeglass in your eye,
And—one coffin when you die, doncherknow.

                  —*Edmund Vance Cooke.*

129
THE JESTER CONDEMNED TO DEATH

One of the Kings of Scanderoon,
  A royal jester
Had in his train, a gross buffoon,
  Who used to pester
The court with tricks inopportune,
Venting on the highest folks his
Scurvy pleasantries and hoaxes
It needs some sense to play the fool,
Which wholesome rule
  Occurred not to our jackanapes,
Who consequently found his freaks
  Lead to innumerable scrapes,
And quite as many tricks and tweaks,
  Which only seemed to make him faster
  Try the patience of his master.

Some in, at last, beyond all measure
Incurred the desperate displeasure
  Of his Serene and raging Highness:
Whether he twitched his most revered
And sacred beard,
  Or had intruded on the shyness
  Of the seraglio, or let fly
  An epigram at royalty,
None knows: his sin was an occult one,
But records tell us that the Sultan,
Meaning to terrify the knave,
  Exclaimed, " 'Tis time to stop that breath;
Thy doom is sealed, presumptuous slave!
  Thou stand'st condemned to certain death:

"Silence, base rebel! no replying!
    But such is my indulgence still,
    That, of my own free grace and will,
I leave to thee the mode of dying."
"Thy royal will be done—'tis just,"
Replied the wretch, and kissed the dust.
    "Since my last moment to assuage,
Your majesty's humane decree
Has deigned to leave the choice to me,
    I'll die, so please you, of old age!"

—*Horace Smith.*

130

ELEGY

The jackals prowl, the serpents hiss
In what was once Persepolis.
Proud Babylon is but a trace
Upon the desert's dusty face.
The topless towers of Ilium
Are ashes. Judah's harp is dumb.
The fleets of Nineveh and Tyre
Are down with Davy Jones, Esquire
And all the oligarchies, kings,
And potentates that rule these things
Are gone! But cheer up; don't be sad;
Think what a lovely time they had!

—*Arthur Guiterman.*

VIII

THE QUESTING STAG

. . . On such a full sea we are now afloat;
And we must take the current when it serves,
Or lose our ventures.

—Shakespeare.

131

WANDERTHIRST

Beyond the East the sunrise, beyond the West the sea,
And East and West the wanderlust that will not not let me be;
It works in me like madness, dear, to bid me say good-bye!
For the seas call and the stars call, and oh, the call of the sky.

I know not where the white road runs, nor what the blue
    hills are,
But man can have the sun for friend, and for his guide a star;
And there's no end of voyaging when once the voice is heard,
For the river calls and the road calls, and oh, the call of a
    bird.

Yonder the long horizon lies, and there by night and day
The old ships draw to home again, and the young ships sail
    away;
And come I may, but go I must, and if men ask you why,
You may put the blame on the stars and the sun and the
    white road and the sky.

—Gerald Gould.

132

GIPSY-HEART

My grandsire was a vagabond
    Who made the Road his pride.
He left his son a wanderer's heart
    And little enough beside;
And all his life my father heard
The fluting of a hidden bird
That lured him on from hedge to hedge
    To walk the world so wide.

And now he walks the worlds beyond
   And drifts on hidden seas
Undesecrated by a chart—
   Blithe derelict at ease.
And sometimes when I halt at night—
In answer to my camp-fire's light
His own uplifts a glowing wedge
   Among the Pleiades.

Women are fair, but all too fond;
   Home holds a man too fast;
I'll choose for mine a freeman's part,
   And sing as I go past.
No lighted windows beckon me,
The open sky my canopy,
I'll camp upon Creation's edge
   A wanderer to the last.

              —*Amelia Josephine Burr*.

133

AT THE CROSSROADS

You to the left and I to the right,
For the ways of men must sever—
And it well may be for a day and a night,
And it well may be forever.
But whether we meet or whether we part
(For our ways are past our knowing),
A pledge from the heart to its fellow heart
On the ways we all are going!
Here's luck!
For we know not where we are going.

We have striven fair in love and war,
But the wheel was always weighted!
We have lost the prize that we struggled for,
We have won the prize that was fated.
We have met our loss with a smile and a song,
And our gains with a wink and a whistle,—
For, whether we're right or whether we're wrong,
There's a rose for every thistle.
Here's luck!
And a drop to wet your whistle!

Whether we win or whether we lose
With the hands that life is dealing,
It is not we nor the ways we choose
But the fall of the cards that's sealing.
There's a fate in love and a fate in fight,
And the best of us all go under—
And whether we're wrong or whether we're right,
We win, sometimes, to our wonder.
Here's luck!
That we may not yet go under!

With a steady swing and an open brow
We have tramped the ways together,
But we're clasping hands at the crossroads now
In the Fiend's own night for weather;
And whether we bleed or whether we smile
In the leagues that lie before us,
The ways of life are many a mile
And the dark of Fate is o'er us.
Here's luck!
And a cheer for the dark before us!

You to the left and I to the right,
For the ways of men must sever,
And it well may be for a day and a night
And it well may be forever!
But whether we live or whether we die
(For the end is past our knowing),
Here's two frank hearts and the open sky,
Be a fair or an ill wind blowing!
Here's luck!
In the teeth of all winds blowing.

—Richard Hovey.

134

THE ROAD TO VAGABONDIA

He was sitting on a doorstep as I went strolling by;
A lonely little beggar with a wistful, homesick eye—
And he wasn't what you'd borrow
And he wasn't what you'd steal—
But I guessed his heart was breaking,
So I whistled him to heel.

They had stoned him through the city streets and naught the
city cared,
But I was heading outward and the roads are sweeter shared,
So I took him for a comrade and I whistled him away—
On the road to Vagabondia that lies across the day.

Yellow dog he was; but bless you—he was just the chap for
me!
For I'd rather have an inch of dog than miles of pedigree
So we stole away together on the road that has no end
With a new-coined day to fling away and all the stars to
spend!

Oh, to walk the road at morning, when the wind is blowing
  clean,
And the yellow daisies fling their gold across a world of
  green—
For the wind it heals the heart-aches and the sun it dries the
  scars,
On the road to Vagabondia that lies beneath the stars.

'Twas the wonder of the going cast a spell about our feet—
We walked because the world was young, because the way
  was sweet;
And we slept in wild-rose meadows by the little wayside
  farms,
'Til the Dawn came up the highroad with the dead moon in
  her arms.

Oh, the Dawn it went before us through a shining lane of
  skies,
And the Dream was at our heartstrings and the light was in
  our eyes,
And we made no boast of glory and we made no boast of
  birth,
On the road to Vagabondia that lies across the earth.

—Dana Burnet.

135

THE RAINBOW'S END

Light of foot and gay of heart,
  He took the rainbow road
With empty pack while others bore
  Ambition's heavy load.

He sought like them the pot of gold,
　But ever on his way
He paused to hear the thrushes sing
　A requiem for the day.

He lingered where hill vistas spread
　New beauty to his sight;
He saw the great hills wear at dawn
　Creation's holy light.

The Autumn's loveliness was his,
　The Spring's ecstatic word;
The lyric phrase of bird and bee
　His listening spirit heard.

He came belated to the place
　Where down the hills descend
The eager feet that seek the gold
　Hung at the rainbow's end.

They found no shining pot of gold
　Who took the trail with him
And never knew his pack of dreams
　Was laden to the brim!

　　　　　　—*Arthur Wallace Peach.*

136

THE VAGABOND

Give to me the life I love,
　Let the lave go by me—
Give the jolly heaven above
　And the byway nigh me.

Bed in the bush with stars to see,
　Bread I dip in the river:
There's the life for a man like me,
　There's the life for ever.

Let the blow fall soon or late,
　Let what will be o'er me;
Give the face of earth around
　And the road before me.
Wealth I seek not, hope nor love,
　Nor a friend to know me;
All I seek, the heaven above
　And the road below me.

Or let autumn fall on me
　Where afield I linger,
Silencing the bird on tree,
　Biting the blue finger:
White as meal the frosty field—
　Warm the fireside haven—
Not to autumn will I yield,
　Not to winter even!

Let the blow fall soon or late,
　Let what will be o'er me;
Give the face of earth around,
　And the road before me.
Wealth I ask not, hope nor love
　Nor a friend to know me.
All I ask the heaven above,
　And the road below me.

—Robert Louis Stevenson.

137

THE SPELL OF THE YUKON

I wanted the gold, and I sought it;
  I scrabbled and mucked like a slave.
Was it famine or scurvy—I fought it;
  I hurled my youth into a grave.
I wanted the gold, and I got it—
  Came out with a fortune last fall,—
Yet somehow life's not what I thought it,
  And somehow the gold isn't all.

No! There's the land—(have you seen it?)
  It's the cussedest land that I know,
From the big, dizzy mountains that screen it
  To the deep, deathlike valleys below.
Some say God was tired when He made it;
  Some say it's a fine land to shun;
Maybe; but there's some as would trade it
  For no land on earth—and I'm one.

You come to get rich (damned good reason);
  You feel like an exile at first;
You hate it like hell for a season,
  And then you are worse that the worst.
It grips you like some kinds of sinning;
  It twists you from foe to a friend;
It seems it's been since the beginning;
  It seems it will be to the end.

I've stood in some mighty-mouthed hollow
  That's plumb-full of hush to the brim;
I've watched the big, husky sun wallow
  In crimson and gold, and grow dim,

Till the moon set the pearly peaks gleaming,
    And the stars tumbled out, neck and crop;
And I thought that I surely was dreaming,
    With the peace o' the world piled on top.

The summer—no sweeter was ever;
    The sunshiny woods all athrill;
The grayling aleap in the river,
    The bighorn asleep on the hill.
The strong life that never knows harness;
    The wilds where the caribou call;
The freshness, the freedom, the farness—
    O God! how I'm stuck on it all!

The winter! the brightness that blinds you,
    The white land locked tight as a drum,
The cold fear that follows and finds you,
    The silence that bludgeons you dumb.
The snows that are older than history,
    The woods where the weird shadows slant;
The stillness, the moonlight, the mystery,
    I've bade 'em good-by—but I can't.

There's a land where the mountains are nameless,
    And the rivers all run God knows where;
There are lives that are erring and aimless,
    And deaths that just hang by a hair;
There are hardships that nobody reckons;
    There are valleys unpeopled and still;
There's a land—oh, it beckons and beckons,
    And I want to go back—and I will.

They're making my money diminish;
    I'm sick of the taste of champagne.
Thank God! when I'm skinned to a finish
    I'll pike to the Yukon again.
I'll fight—and you bet it's no sham-fight;
    It's hell!—but I've been there before;
And it's better than this by a damsight—
    So me for the Yukon once more.

There's gold, and it's haunting and haunting;
    It's luring me on as of old;
Yet it isn't the gold that I'm wanting
    So much as just finding the gold.
It's the great, big, broad land 'way up yonder,
    It's the forests where silence has lease;
It's the beauty that thrills me with wonder,
    It's the stillness that fills me with peace.

                           —*Robert W. Service.*

138

DESERT BORN

Yes, I have known the tragedy a desert life can give;
Yet there is not another place where I would rather live.
I've known the desolation of desert miles to cross
A-burning up with thirstiness, and leading my lame hoss.
I've felt the clutch of cactus a-tearing at my clothes,
The yellow sun a-scorching me and blistering my nose.
And I've been sunk in hopelessness a-lying 'neath night skies
With sand and sweat and hungriness a-eating out my eyes.

Yes, I have seen companions wilt in desert's cruel hand;
And I have helped to lay them there in desert's greedy sand.

My soul's been bent with gnawing grief for loved ones I have
   lost
Whose very spirits burned away at such a tragic cost.
I've felt the years a-wearing me with things I can't explain;
I'm always poor in worldly goods, and never worked for gain.
I've tried to live in other spots where there is ease and rest;
But something always brings me to the place I love the best.

Now, maybe it's the whitish stars that fleck the purple night;
Or maybe it's the desert burs that stick so awful tight;
Or maybe it's the silences that fill the desert years;
Or maybe it's the lonesomeness, the tragedy and tears.
Or maybe it's the speechless mounds in cactus' scanty shade
Where I have knelt in desert sand and reverently prayed.
But when I come to think of it as back again I go—
Why, maybe it's the—maybe it's—Dog-gone-it, I don't know!
                              —*Marie Taggart Keith.*

139

VACATION

It seems to me I'd like to go
Where bells don't ring, nor whistles blow,
Nor clocks don't strike, nor gongs don't sound,
And I'd have stillness all around.
No real stillness, but just the tree's
Low whispering, or the hum of bees,
Or brooks' faint babbling over stones
In strangely, softly tangled tones,
Or maybe a cricket or katydid,
Or the song of birds in hedges hid,
Or just such sweet sounds as these
To fill the tired heart with ease.

If 'tweren't for sight and sound and smell
I'd like a city pretty well,
But when it comes to getting rest
I like the country lots the best.
Sometimes it seems to me I must
Just quit the city's din and dust
And get out where the sky is blue;
And say, how does it seem to you?

—Eugene Field.

140

THE CALL

Did you ever have a longin' to get out and buck the trail,
And to face the crashin' lightnin' and the thunder and the
     gale?
Not for no partic'lar reason but to give the world the laugh,
And to show the roarin' elyments you still can stand the gaff.

Don't you ever feel a yearnin' just to try your luck again
Down the rippin' plungin' rapids with a bunch of reg'lar
     men?
Don't you ever sorta hanker for a rough and risky trip,
Just to prove you're still a livin' and you haven't lost your
     grip?

Can't you hear the woods a-callin' for to have another try
Sleepin' out beneath the spruces with a roof of moonlit sky,
With the wind a sorta singin' through the branches overhead
And your fire a gaily crackin' and your pipe a-glowin' red?

Don't you often get to feelin' sorta cramped and useless there,
Makin' figgers and a-shinin' your pants upon a chair?
Don't you yearn to get acquainted once again with Life and
  God?
If you don't, then Heaven help you, for you're dyin' in yer
  pod.

—Earl H. Emmons.

IX

THE STAG AS NATURE'S NOBLEMAN

The world is too much with us; late and soon,

Getting and spending, we lay waste our powers:

Little we see in Nature that is ours . . .

—*William Wordsworth.*

141

THE HAPPIEST HEART

Who drives the horses of the sun
Shall lord it but a day;
Better the lowly deed were done,
And kept the humble way.

The rust will find the sword of fame,
The dust will hide the crown;
Ay, none shall nail so high his name
Time will not tear it down.

The happiest heart that ever beat
Was in some quiet breast
That found the common daylight sweet,
And left to Heaven the rest.

—*John Vance Cheney.*

142

"GRATIAS AGO"

Since of earth, air and water,
The gods have made me part—
Let every human sin be mine
Except the thankless heart!
Privileged greatly, I partake
Of sleep and death and birth;
And kneeling, drink the sacrament—
The good red wine of earth.

I shall not ask the High Gods
For aught that they can give;

They gave the greatest gift of all
When first they bade me live.
Great gift of dawn and starlight,
Of sea and grass and river;
With leave to toil and laugh and weep
And praise the Sun forever!

Be death the end or not the end,
Too richly blest am I
To seek the hill behind the hill,
The sky behind the sky.
Let the red earth that bore me
Give me her call again,
And I'll lie still beneath her flowers
And sleep and not complain.

Let those the gods have blinded
Hold their long feud with Fate—
And clutch at toys that never yet
Could make one mean man great.
Let those that Earth has bastarded
Fret and contrive and plan—
But I will enter like an heir
The old estate of man!

—*Geoffrey Howard.*

143

THE PIONEER

Long years ago I blazed a trail
　Through lovely woods unknown till then
And marked with cairns of splintered shale
　A mountain way for other men;

For other men who came and came:
  They trod the path more plain to see,
They gave my trail another's name
  And no one speaks or knows of me.

The trail runs high, the trail runs low
  Where windflowers dance or columbine;
The scars are healed that long ago
  My ax cut deep on birch and pine.

Another's name my trail may bear,
  But still I keep, in waste and wood,
My joy because the trail is there,
  My peace because the trail is good.
                          —*Arthur Guiterman.*

144

OUT WHERE THE WEST BEGINS

Out where the handclasp's a little stronger,
Out where the smile dwells a little longer,
  That's where the West begins;
Out where the sun is a little brighter,
Where the snows that fall are a trifle whiter,
Where the bonds of home are a wee bit tighter,
  That's where the West begins.

Out where the skies are a trifle bluer,
Out where friendship's a little truer,
  That's where the West begins;
Out where a fresher breeze is blowing,
Where there's laughter in every streamlet flowing,
Where there's more of reaping and less of sowing,
  That's where the West begins.

Out where the world is in the making,
Where fewer hearts in despair are aching,
    That's where the West begins;
Where there's more of singing and less of sighing,
Where there's more of giving and less of buying,
And a man makes friends without half trying—
    That's where the West begins.

                    —*Arthur Chapman.*

145

THE PRAIRIES

    These are the gardens of the Desert, these
The unshorn fields, boundless and beautiful,
For which the speech of England has no name—
The Prairies. I behold them for the first,
And my heart swells, while the dilated sight
Takes in the encircling vastness. Lo! they stretch,
In airy undulations, far away,
As if the ocean, in his gentlest swell,
Stood still, with all his rounded billows fixed,
And motionless forever.—Motionless?—
No—they are all unchained again. The clouds
Sweep over with their shadows, and, beneath,
The surface rolls and fluctuates to the eye;
Dark hollows seem to glide along and chase
The sunny ridges. Breezes of the South!
Who toss the golden and the flame-like flowers,
And pass the prairie-hawk that, poised on high
Flaps his broad wings, yet moves not—ye have played
Among the palms of Mexico and vines
Of Texas, and have crisped the limpid brooks
That from the fountains of Sonora glide

Into the calm Pacific—have ye fanned
A nobler or a lovelier scene than this?
Man hath no power in all this glorious work:
The hand that built the firmament hath heaved
And smoothed these verdant swells, and sown their slopes
With herbage, planted them with island groves,
And hedged them round with forests. Fitting floor
For this magnificent temple of the sky—
With flowers whose glory and whose multitude
Rival the constellations! The great heavens
Seem to stoop down upon the scene in love,—
A nearer vault, and of a tenderer blue,
Than that which bends above our eastern hills . . .

   As o'er the verdant waste I guide my steed,
Among the high rank grass that sweeps his sides
The hollow beating of his footstep seems
A sacrilegious sound. I think of those
Upon whose rest he tramples. Are they here—
The dead of other days?—and did the dust
Of these fair solitudes once stir with life
And burn with passion? Let the mighty mounds
That overlook the rivers, or that rise
In the dim forest crowded with old oaks,
Answer. A race, that long has passed away,
Built them;—a disciplined and populous race
Heaped, with long toil, the earth, while yet the Greek
Was hewing the Pentelicus to forms
Of symmetry, and rearing on its rock
The glittering Parthenon. These ample fields
Nourished their harvests, here their herds were fed,
When haply by their stalls the bison lowed,
And bowed his manèd shoulder to the yoke.
All day this desert murmured with their toils,

Till twilight blushed, and lovers walked, and wooed
In a forgotten language, and old tunes,
From instruments of unremembered form,
Gave the soft winds a voice. The red man came—
The roaming hunter tribes, warlike and fierce,
And the mound-builders vanished from the earth.
The solitude of centuries untold
Has settled where they dwelt. The prairie-wolf
Hunts in their meadows, and his fresh-dug pen
Yawns by my path. The gopher mines the ground
Where stood their swarming cities. All is gone;
All—save the piles of earth that hold their bones,
The platforms where they worshipped unknown gods,
The barriers which they builded from the soil
To keep the foe at bay—'til o'er the walls
The wild beleaguerers broke, and, one by one,
The strongholds of the plain were forced, and heaped
With corpses. The brown vultures of the wood
Flocked to those vast uncovered sepulchres,
And sat unscared and silent at their feast.
Haply some solitary fugitive,
Lurking in marsh and forest, till the sense
Of desolation and of fear became
Bitterer than death, yielded himself to die.
Man's better nature triumphed then. Kind words
Welcomed and soothed him; the rude conquerors
Seated the captive with their chiefs; he chose
A bride among their maidens, and at length
Seemed to forget—yet ne'er forgot—the wife
Of his first love, and her sweet little ones,
Butchered, amid their shrieks, with all his race.

Thus change the forms of being. Thus arise
Races of living things, glorious in strength,

And perish, as the quickening breath of God
Fills them, or is withdrawn. The red man, too,
Has left the blooming wilds he ranged so long,
And, nearer to the Rocky Mountains, sought
A wilder hunting-ground. The beaver builds
No longer by these streams, but far away,
On waters whose blue surface ne'er gave back
The white man's face—among Missouri's springs,
And pools whose issues swell the Oregon—
He rears his little Venice. In these plains
The bison feeds no more. Twice twenty leagues
Beyond remotest smoke of hunter's camp,
Roams the majestic brute, in herds that shake
The earth with thundering steps—yet here I meet
His ancient footprints stamped beside the pool.

    Still this great solitude is quick with life.
Myriads of insects, gaudy as the flowers
They flutter over, gentle quadrupeds,
And birds, that scarce have learned the fear of man,
Are here, and sliding reptiles of the ground,
Startlingly beautiful. The graceful deer
Bounds to the wood at my approach. The bee,
A more adventurous colonist than man,
With whom he came across the eastern deep,
Fills the savannas with his murmurings,
And hides his sweets, as in the golden age,
Within the hollow oak. I listen long
To his domestic hum, and think I hear
The sound of that advancing multitude
Which soon shall fill these deserts. From the ground
Comes up the laugh of children, the soft voice
Of maidens, and the sweet and solemn hymn
Of Sabbath worshippers. The low of herds

Blends with the rustling of the heavy grain
Over the dark brown furrows. All at once
A fresher wind sweeps by, and breaks my dream,
And I am in the wilderness alone.

                                    —*William Cullen Bryant.*

146

"HE DONE HIS DAMDEST"

I ask that when my spirit quits this shell of mortal clay
And o'er the trail across the range pursues its silent way,
That no imposing marble shaft may mark the spot where rest
The tailings of the bard who sang the praises of the West.
But, that above them may be placed a slab of white or gray,
And on it but the epitaph carved in the earlier day,
Upon the headboard of a man who did the best he could
To have the bad deeds of his life o'ershadowed by the good:
          "He Done His Damdest."

Engrave upon the polished face of that plain, simple stone,
No nicely worded sentiment intended to condone
The sins of an eventful life, nor say the virtues wiped
Away the stains of vice—in lines original or swiped;
That rough but honest sentiment that stood above the head
Of one who wore his boots into his final earthly bed
Is good enough for me to have above my mould'ring clay—
Just give the name and day I quit and underneath it say:
          "He Done His Damdest."

Some who are overstocked with phony piety may raise
Their hands in blank amazement at the sentiment and gaze
Upon the simple marble slab 'neath which the sleeper lies,
With six or seven different kinds of horror in their eyes;

But hardy sons and daughters of this brave and rugged West
Will see a tribute in the line so pointedly expressed—
And what more earnest tribute could be paid to any man
Whose weary feet have hit the trail towards the Mystery,
    than:

        "He Done His Damdest."
                    —*E. Bell Guthrey.*

147

THE MOUNTAINS ARE A LONELY FOLK

The mountains they are silent folk,
   They stand afar—alone;
And the clouds that kiss their brows at night
   Hear neither sigh nor groan.
Each bears him in his ordered place
   As soldiers do, and bold and high
They fold their forests round their feet
   And bolster up the sky.
                —*Hamlin Garland.*

148

DO YOU FEAR THE WIND?

Do you fear the force of the wind,
   The slash of the rain?
Go face them and fight them,
   Be savage again.
Go hungry and cold like the wolf,
   Go wade like the crane:

The palms of your hands will thicken
The skin of your cheek will tan,
You'll grow ragged and weary and swarthy,
    But you'll walk like a man!
                    —*Hamlin Garland.*

149

LASCA

I want free life and I want fresh air,
I long for the canter after the cattle,
The crack of the whips like shot in battle,
The medley of horns and hoofs and heads
That wars and wrangles and scatters and spreads
The green beneath and the blue above,
The dash and danger, life, love—and Lasca.

Lasca used to ride on a mouse-gray mustang close to my
    side,
With blue serape and bright-belled spur,
Why! I laughed with joy as I looked at her;
Little she knew of books or creeds,
An Ave Maria sufficed her needs;
Little she cared save to be at my side,
To ride with me and ever to ride,
From San Sabras shore to Lavaca's tide
In Texas, down by the Rio Grande.

Her eyes were brown—a deep, deep brown,
Her hair was darker than her eye,
Something in her smile and frown
Curled crimson lips and instep high,

Showed that there ran in each blue vein
Mixed with the milder Aztec strain
The vigorous vintage of old Spain.
She was alive in every limb
With feeling to her finger tips.
And when the sun is like a fire
And the sky one burning blue sapphire
One does not drink in little sips
In Texas, down by the Rio Grande.

She was as bold as the billows that beat,
She was as wild as the breezes that blow.
From her little head to her little feet,
She was swayed in her suppleness to and fro
By each gust of passion. A sapling pine
That grows on the edge of a Kansas bluff
And wars with the wind when the weather is rough
Is like this Lasca—this love of mine.
Why she would hunger that I might live,
She'd take the bitter and leave me the sweet.

But once when I made her jealous for fun
With something I whispered, or looked, or done,
One Sunday in San Antonio to a glorious girl on the
    Alamo,
She drew from her garter a slim little dagger
And—sting of a wasp—it made me stagger.
An inch to the left or an inch to the right,
And I shouldn't be maundering here tonight.
But she sobbed, and sobbing so swiftly bound
Her torn rabaso about the wound,
That I quite forgave her. Scratches don't count
In Texas, down by the Rio Grande.

The air was heavy, the night was hot,
I sat by her side and forgot—forgot,
Forgot that the herd was taking its rest,
Forgot that the air was close, oppressed,
That the Texas Northers comes sudden and soon,
In the dead of night, or the blaze of noon,
And once let the herd at its breath take fright
And nothing on earth can stop its flight.
And woe to the rider and woe to the steed
That falls in front of that mad stampede.

Was that thunder? No, by the Lord.
I sprang to my saddle without a word.
One foot on mine, she clung behind,
Away on a mad chase down the wind.
Never was horse pressed half so hard,
Never was steed so little spared,
For we rode for our lives,
And you shall hear how we fared
In Texas, down by the Rio Grande.

The mustang flew and we urged him on,
There's one chance left, and you have but one,
Halt! Jump to the earth and shoot your horse,
Crouch under his carcass and take your chance,
And if the steers in their frantic course
Don't batter you both to pieces at once
You may thank your stars.—If not, good-bye
To the quickening kiss and the long drawn sigh
In Texas, down by the Rio Grande.

The cattle gained on us just as I felt
My old six-shooter behind in my belt.
Down came the mustang, down came we,

Clinging together. What was the rest?
A body that spread itself over my breast,
Two arms that shielded my dizzy head,
Two lips that close to my lips were pressed,
As over us surged the sea of steers,
Blows that beat blood to my eyes and ears.
When I could rise—Lasca was dead.

I gouged out a grave a few feet deep
And there in earth's arms I laid her to sleep,
Where she is lying, no one knows.
The summer shines and the winter snows.
For many a year the flowers have spread
A pall of petals above her head.
The little grey hawk hangs aloft in the air,
The sly coyote trots here and there,
The rattlesnake glides, and glitters, and slides
Into a rift in the cottonwood tree.

The buzzard sails on, and comes and is gone,
Stately and still like a ship at sea.
And I wonder why I do not care
For the things that are and the things that were.
Ah, half my heart lies buried there
In Texas, down by the Rio Grande.

150

EARTH VICTORY

How stubbornly I cleared the field
And pulverized the stony land
And watered all its sterile sand
To make the barren acres yield.

But when I gained the victory
And moulded to my will the ground,
I rested from my work and found
The subtle earth had moulded me.
                    —*Lewis Morgan.*

X

THE STAG AT SEA

The wind is piping loud, my boys,
  The lightning flashing free;
While the hollow oak our palace is,
  Our heritage the sea.

  —*Allan Cunningham.*

A WET SHEET AND A FLOWING SEA

A wet sheet and a flowing sea,
    A wind that follows fast,
And fills the white and rustling sail,
    And bends the gallant mast—
And bends the gallant mast, my boys,
    While, like the eagle free,
Away the good ship flies, and leaves
    Old England on the lee.

"O for a soft and gentle mind!"
    I heard a fair one cry;
But give to me the snoring breeze
    And white waves heaving high—
And white waves heaving high, my boys,
    The good ship tight and free;
The world of waters is our home,
    And merry men are we.

There's tempest in yon hornèd moon,
    And lightning in yon cloud;
And hark the music, mariners!
    The wind is piping loud—
The wind is piping loud, my boys,
    The lightning flashing free;
While the hollow oak our palace is,
    Our heritage the sea.
                    —*Allan Cunningham.*

152

DERELICT

"Fifteen Men on the Dead Man's Chest—" As a youngster
that line doubtless intrigued you. Calculating the limitations
of the human torso, you may have wondered, vaguely, how
so many contrived to congregate on such a limited sphere.
Or perhaps it was a treasure chest, and the fifteen were met
to jubilate a piratical victory.

Both surmises are inaccurate. The Dead Man's Chest is a
treacherous, little-known reef in the Caribbean Sea. It was
this locale that Robert Louis Stevenson had in mind when he
penned the immortal quatrain. (Lloyd Osbourne, Stevenson's
stepson, for whom *Treasure Island* was written, declares that
the lines were entirely original with Stevenson, and not, as
commonly supposed, the chorus of a venerable sea chantey.)

Like many another, Young Ewing Allison, Louisville news-
paper man, became fascinated with the grisly fragment; de-
termined to fashion a complete poem on the theme. The result was his *Derelict*, which is here reproduced in full.
Though nestling in many a private collection, it has not been
printed as frequently as its excellence deserves.

Basis of Mr. Allison's poem is a seventeenth-century legend
of a treasure-laden Spanish galleon, raided by a pirate crew.
All on board were forced to walk the plank. The pirates then
fell to fighting amongst themselves. Fifteen of the lot forced
their companions into the long boat; set them adrift on the
open sea. Still unable to make peaceful division of the loot,
the huskies continued quarreling. The galleon drifted, derelict, on Dead Man's Chest, where it was ultimately dis-
covered by members of the crew who had been set adrift.
The poem begins where one of the group relates the sight
that met their eyes as they boarded the vessel.

The poem, as first written, contained three stanzas, and
was known as *A Piratical Ballad*. It was composed in 1891—
three years before Stevenson's death, but he was never privileged to see it. Allison worked on his masterpiece, polishing
it with care, over a period of nearly forty years. He was

never completely satisfied with the result; intended to add another stanza, bringing in Captain Flint's parrot, with its raucous cry, "Pieces of Eight!" The version printed here is from a manuscript incorporating the author's final alterations. Young Ewing Allison died in 1932, aged 79.

Fifteen men on the Dead Man's Chest—
    Yo-ho-ho and a bottle of rum!
Drink and the devil had done for the rest—
    Yo-ho-ho and a bottle of rum!
The mate was fixed by the bos'n's pike,
The bos'n brained with a marlinspike,
And Cookey's throat was marked belike
      It had been gripped
      By fingers ten
      And there they lay,
      All good dead men
Like break o' day in a boozing ken—
    Yo-ho-ho and a bottle of rum!

Fifteen men of a whole ship's list—
    Yo-ho-ho and a bottle of rum!
Dead and bedamned, and the rest gone whist—
    Yo-ho-ho and a bottle of rum!
The skipper lay with his nob in gore
Where the scullion's axe his cheek had shore—
And the scullion he was stabbed times four.
      And there they lay,
      And the soggy skies
      Dripped all day long
      In up-staring eyes—
At murk sunset and at foul sunrise—
    Yo-ho-ho and a bottle of rum!

Fifteen men of 'em stiff and stark—
  Yo-ho-ho and a bottle of rum!
Ten of the crew had the murder mark—
  Yo-ho-ho and a bottle of rum!
'Twas a cutlass swipe, or an ounce of lead,
Or a yawning hole in a battered head,
And the scuppers glut with a rotting red,
      And there they lay—
      Aye, damn my eyes!—
      All lookouts clapped
      On paradise—
All souls bound just contrariwise—
  Yo-ho-ho and a bottle of rum!

Fifteen men of 'em good and true—
  Yo-ho-ho and a bottle of rum!
Every man jack could ha' sailed with Old Pew—
  Yo-ho-ho and a bottle of rum!
There was chest on chest full of Spanish gold,
With a ton of plate in the middle hold,
And the cabins riot of stuff untold.
      And they lay there
      That had took the plum,
      With sightless glare
      And their lips struck dumb,
While we shared all by the rule of thumb—
  Yo-ho-ho and a bottle of rum!

More was seen through the sternlight screen—
  Yo-ho-ho and a bottle of rum!
Chartings ondoubt where a woman had been—
  Yo-ho-ho and a bottle of rum!
A flimsy shift on a bunker cot,
With a thin dirk slot through the bosom spot

And the lace stiff-dry in a purplish blot.
    Or was she wench . . .
    Or some shuddering maid . . . ?
    That dared the knife
    And that took the blade!
By God! She was stuff for a plucky jade—
    Yo-ho-ho and a bottle of rum!

Fifteen men on the Dead Man's Chest—
    Yo-ho-ho and a bottle of rum!
Drink and the devil had done for the rest—
    Yo-ho-ho and a bottle of rum!
We wrapped them all in a mains'l tight,
With twice ten turns of the hawser's bight,
And we heaved 'em over and out of sight—
    With a yo-heave-ho!
    And a fare-you-well!
    And a sullen plunge
    In the sullen swell—
Ten fathoms deep on the road to hell—
    Yo-ho-ho and a bottle of rum!

             —Young Ewing Allison.

Shortly before his death, in 1916, James Whitcomb Riley, who referred to the poem as "a masterly and exquisite ballad of delicious horrificness," wrote a parody stanza, in which he paid tribute to the author:

Fifteen men on the Dead Man's Chest
    Yo-ho-ho and a bottle of rum!
Young E. Allison done all the rest,
    Yo-ho-ho and a bottle of rum!

He's sung this song for you and me,
  Jest as it wuz—or ort to be—
Clean through time and eternity,
  Yo-ho-ho and a bottle of rum!

153

ANNABEL LEE

It was many and many a year ago,
  In the kingdom by the sea,
That a maiden there lived whom you may know
  By the name of Annabel Lee;
And this maiden she lived with no other thought
  Than to love and be loved by me.

I was a child and *she* was a child,
  In this kingdom by the sea,
But we loved with a love that was more than love,
  I and my Annabel Lee;
With a love that the winged seraphs of heaven
  Coveted her and me.

And this was the reason that, long ago,
  In this kingdom by the sea,
A wind blew out of a cloud, chilling
  My beautiful Annabel Lee;
So that her highborn kinsmen came
  And bore her away from me,
To shut her up in a sepulchre
  In this kingdom by the sea.

The angels, not half so happy in heaven,
    Went envying her and me;
Yes! that was the reason (as all men know,
    In this kingdom by the sea)
That the wind came out of the cloud by night,
    Chilling and killing my Annabel Lee.

But our love it was stronger by far than the love
    Of those who were older than we,
    Of many far wiser than we;
And neither the angels in heaven above,
    Nor the demons down under the sea,
Can ever dissever my soul from the soul
    Of the beautiful Annabel Lee:
For the moon never beams, without bringing me dreams
    Of the beautiful Annabel Lee;

And the stars never rise, but I see the bright eyes
    Of the beautiful Annabel Lee;
And so, all the night-tide, I lie down by the side
Of my darling—my darling—my life and my bride,
    In her sepulchre there by the sea,
    In her tomb by the sounding sea.

                  —*Edgar Allan Poe.*

154

THE BALLAD OF THE IVANHOE

"What is she making?" asked the mate;
    "She's making her sixteen, sir."
"One hundred days to the Golden Gate,"
    Said the hard-case mate,—
    The *Ivanhoe* was running for the open sea.

"What's she making?" asked the skipper;
  "Still logging her sixteen, sir."
"Two more nights and she'll lose the dipper,"
  Muttered the skipper,—
  And the *Ivanhoe* was whooping it southerly.

"What's she makin', bullies?" asked Chips;
  "Sixteen knots on her course, lad."
"Then she'll whip them lubberly London ships,"
  Grinned Carpenter Chips.—
  And then the Pampero caught her under full sail.

"She's lost one whole storm suit," said Sails,
  They fetched new from the locker,
And dressed her from boom to her spanker brails
  For the Cape Horn gales,—
  And then old *Ivanhoe* went southing toward the Horn.

"Seen no sun in a month," growled Bose,
  "A full Horn gale's a-blowin',
"An' all of yer yards is jammed up close,
  My Gawd!—'ow it snows!"
  Old *Ivanhoe* had been a full four weeks off Stiff.

"Where's the skipper?" the froze mate said,
  "I haven't seen him of late."
"He's overboard, and he's drowned and dead,"
  And, shaking his head,
  "You'll have to sail her to 'Frisco," said the second.

"Wot was it crashed in the black night?"
  "Her topmasts carried away!"

"My word, but ain't it blowin' a fright?
  Oh, Gawd fer th' light!"
And that was when she's been six weeks off old Cape
    Stiff.

Six men lay dead. Calm came in spells.
  The second mate went crazy;
Old *Ivanhoe* lifted to the swells
  Changing both her bells,—
  Her wreckage trailed astern amidst the Cape Horn
    bergs.

"What is she making?" asked the mate.
  "Just creeping at two knots, sir."
"Three hundred days to the Golden Gate,"
  Said her hard-case mate,—
  When a fair wind blew after eight weeks off Cape
    Stiff.

"Will we sail into Vallapo
  For refittin'?" asked the hands.
"No sons! Not by a hell of a show!
  We will take her so,
  Just as she is, to 'Frisco, said her hard-case mate.

"A steamer's comin' through the swell,
  Offerin' us assistance."
"Signal the lubber to go to hell!
  Signal him, 'All's well.'"
  Old *Ivanhoe* had been two hundred days at sea.

"What's come of that old *Ivanhoe*?"
  Asked one of the clerks at Lloyd's,

"Perished, maybe, in a Cape Horn blow,
　　There's none to know!"
An then they slowly tolled the bell for her at Lloyd's.

Jury rigged, with all her freight,
　　And the red rust on her sides,
Came *Ivanhoe*, a twelvemonth late,
　　With her hard-case mate,
　　And half her crew, slow stealing through the Golden
　　Gate.

　　　　　　　　　　　　　　　　　—*Bill Adams.*

155

THE YARN OF THE "NANCY BELL"

'Twas on the shores that round our coast
　　From Deal to Ramsgate span,
That I found alone on a piece of stone
　　An elderly naval man.

His hair was weedy, his beard was long,
　　And weedy and long was he,
And I heard this wight on the shore recite,
　　In a singular minor key:

"Oh, I am a cook and the captain bold,
　　And the mate of the *Nancy* brig,
And a bo'sun tight, and a midshipmite,
　　And the crew of the captain's gig."

And he shook his fists and he tore his hair,
　Till I really felt afraid,
For I couldn't help thinking the man had been
　drinking,
　And so I simply said:

"Oh, elderly man, it's little I know
　Of the duties of men of the sea,
And I'll eat my hand if I understand
　How you can possibly be

"At once a cook, and a captain bold,
　And the mate of the *Nancy* brig,
And a bo'sun tight, and a midshipmite,
　And the crew of the captain's gig."

Then he gave a hitch to his trousers, which
　Is a trick all seamen larn,
And having got rid of a thumping quid,
　He spun his painful yarn:

"'Twas in the good ship *Nancy Bell*
　That we sailed to the Indian Sea,
And there on a reef we come to grief,
　Which has often occurred to me.

"And pretty nigh all the crew was drowned
　(There was seventy-seven o' soul),
And only ten of the *Nancy's* men
　Said 'here' to the muster-roll.

"There was me and the cook and the captain bold,
　And the mate of the *Nancy* brig,
And the bo'sun tight, and a midshipmite,
　And the crew of the captain's gig.

"For a month we'd neither wittles nor drunk,
    Till a-hungry we did feel,
So we drawed a lot, and accordin' shot
    The captain for our meal.

"The next lot fell to the *Nancy's* mate,
    And a delicate dish he made;
Then our appetite with the midshipmite
    We seven survivors stayed.

"And then we murdered the bo'sun tight,
    And he much resembled pig;
Then we wittled free, did the cook and me,
    On the crew of the captain's gig.

"Then only the cook and me was left,
    And the delicate question, 'Which
Of us two goes to the kettle?' arose,
    And we argued it out as sich.

"For I loved that cook as a brother, I did,
    And the cook he worshipped me;
But we'd both be blowed if we'd either be **stowed**
    In the other chap's hold, you see.

" 'I'll be eat if you dines off me,' says Tom.
    'Yes, that,' says I, 'you'll be,—
I'm boiled if I die, my friend,' quoth I.
    And 'Exactly so,' quoth he.

"Says he, 'Dear James, to murder me
    Were a foolish thing to do,
For don't you see that you can't cook *me*,
    While I can—and will—cook *you!*'

"So he boils the water, and takes the salt
   And the pepper in portions true
(Which he never forgot), and some chopped shalot,
   And some sage and parsley too.

" 'Come here,' says he, with a proper pride,
   Which his smiling features tell,
' 'Twill soothing be if I let you see
   How extremely nice you'll smell.'

"And he stirred it round and round and round,
   And he sniffed at the foaming froth;
When I ups with his heels, and smothers his squeals
   In the scum of the boiling broth.

"And I eat that cook in a week or less,
   And—as I eating be
The last of his chops, why, I almost drops,
   For a vessel in sight I see.

"And I never larf, and I never smile,
   And I never lark or play,
But sit and croak, and a single joke
   I have,—which is to say:

"Oh, I am a cook and a captain bold,
   And the mate of the *Nancy* brig,
And a bo'sun tight, and a midshipmite,
   And the crew of the captain's gig."
                —*W. S. Gilbert.*

156

THE DECKHANDS

There's some is bums from city slums
That ain't so strong on knowledge;
There's some that hails from county jails
An' some that hails from college;
There's some is mild an' some is wild
An' some is smart an' chipper—
The kind that climbs an' gets, sometimes,
To be a mate or skipper.

   A lousy lot
   You'll say, an' not
What you'd consider what is what;
   Well, yes, we lack
   A high shellac
But we're not meant for bric-à-brac.

   Believe me, pard, we're rough and hard
An' scarcely things of beauty;
We're never made for dress parade
But just for heavy duty;
To strain our spines at handlin' lines—
To do our stint of swabbin'—
When combers roll to pass the coal
To keep the screws a-throbbin'.

   It's true we ain't
   Exactly "quaint"
Like "hale old salts" the painters paint,
   But we can do
   The work for you—
An' that's the business of a crew.

We're single guys without no ties
Of any kind to bind us,
Tho' I can't state the aggregate
Of girls we've left behind us.
In port we drink an' get in "clink"
In spite of ev'ry warnin'—
Our money spent, we're all content
To ship again next mornin'.

The mate may rare
An' swear an' tear—
Us deckhands doesn't greatly care,
For kicks an' blame
Is in the game—
They've got to have us just the same.

November blows an' wintry snows
Don't find us any glummer,
We still can shirk our daily work
As well as in the summer.
For, so we gets our cigarettes
An' wages, when it's over
We'll take a trip in any ship
An' think ourselves in clover.

We wouldn't please
At balls or teas,
Where high-toned folks is what you sees;
But don't you doubt
This fact, old scout,
We're guys they can't get on without.

—Anonymous.

157
THE LINER SHE'S A LADY

The Liner she's a lady, an' she never looks nor 'eeds—
The Man-o'-War's 'er 'usband, an' 'e gives 'er all she needs;
But, oh, the little cargo-boats, that sail the wet seas roun'.
They're just the same as you an' me a-plyin' up an' down!

Plyin' up an' down, Jenny, 'angin' round the Yard,
All the way by Fratton tram down to Portsmouth 'Ard;
Anythin' for business, an' we're growin' old—
Plyin' up an' down, Jenny, waitin' in the cold!

The Liner she's a lady by the paint upon 'er face,
An' if she meets an accident they count it sore disgrace.
The Man-o'-War's 'er 'usband, and 'e's always 'andy by,
But, oh, the little cargo-boats, they've got to load or die!

The Liner she's a lady, and 'er route is cut an' dried;
The Man-o'-War's 'er 'usband, an' 'e always keeps beside;
But, oh, the little cargo-boats that 'aven't any man,
They've got to do their business first, and make the most they
    can!

The Liner she's a lady, and if a war should come,
The Man-o'-War's 'er 'usband, and 'e'd bid 'er stay at home;
But, oh, the little cargo-boats that fill with every tide!
'E'd 'ave to up an' fight for them for they are England's pride.

The Liner she's a lady, but if she wasn't made,
There still would be the cargo-boats for 'ome an' foreign
    trade.
The Man-o'-War's 'er 'usband, but if we wasn't 'ere,
'E wouldn't have to fight at all for 'ome an' friends so dear.

'Ome an' friends so dear, Jenny, 'angin' round the Yard,
All the way by Fratton tram down to Portsmouth 'Ard;
Anythin' for business, an' we're growin' old—
'Ome an' friends so dear, Jenny, waitin' in the cold!

—*Rudyard Kipling.*

158

THE SAILOR'S CONSOLATION

One night came on a hurricane,
   The sea was mountains rolling,
When Barney Buntline turned his quid,
   And said to Billy Bowling:
"A strong nor-wester's blowing, Bill;
   Hark! don't ye hear it roar, now?
Lord help 'em, how I pities them
   Unhappy folks on shore now!

"Foolhardy chaps who live in towns,
   What danger they are all in,
And now lie quaking in their beds,
   For fear the roof should fall in;
Poor creatures! how they envies us,
   And wishes, I've a notion,
For our good luck, in such a storm,
   To be upon the ocean!

"And as for them who're out all day
   On business from their houses,
And late at night are coming home,
   To cheer their babes and spouses,—

While you and I, Bill, on the deck
  Are comfortably lying,
My eyes! what tiles and chimney-pots
  About their heads are flying!

"And very often have we heard
  How men are killed and undone
By overturns of carriages,
  By thieves, and fires in London;
We know what risks all landsmen run,
  From noblemen to tailors;
Then, Bill, let us thank Providence
  That you and I are sailors."
                    —*Charles Dibdin.*

159

A SAILOR'S YARN

This is the tale that was told to me,
By a battered and shattered son of the sea—
To me and my messmate, Silas Green,
When I was a guileless young marine.

" 'Twas the good ship *Gyascutus,*
  All in the China seas,
With the wind a-lee and the capstan free
  To catch the summer breeze.

" 'Twas Captain Porgie on the deck,
  To his mate in the mizzen hatch,
While the boatswain bold, in the forward hold,
  Was winding the larboard watch.

" 'Oh, how does our good ship head to-night?
　　How heads our gallant craft?'
'Oh, she heads to the E.S.W. by N.,
　　And the binnacle lies abaft!'

" 'Oh, what does the quadrant indicate,
　　And how does the sextant stand?'
'Oh, the sextant's down to the freezing point,
　　And the quadrant's lost a hand!'

" 'Oh, and if the quadrant has lost a hand,
　　And the sextant falls so low,
It's our bodies and bones to Davy Jones
　　This night are bound to go!

" 'Oh, fly aloft to the garboard strake!
　　And reef the spanker boom;
Bend a studding sail on the martingale,
　　To give her weather room.

" 'Oh, boatswain, down in the for'ard hold
　　What water do you find?'
'Four foot and a half by the royal gaff
　　And rather more behind!'

" 'Oh, sailors, collar your marline spikes
　　And each belaying pin;
Come stir your stumps, and spike the pumps,
　　Or more will be coming in!'

"They stirred their stumps, they spiked the
　　pumps,
　　They spliced the mizzen brace;
Aloft and alow they worked, but oh!
　　The water gained space.

"They bored a hole above the keel
  To let the water out;
But, strange to say, to their dismay,
  The water in did spout.

"Then up spoke the Cook of our gallant ship,
  And he was a lubber brave:
'I have several wives in various ports,
  And my life I'd orter save.'

"Then up spoke the Captain of Marines,
  Who dearly loved his prog:
'It's awful to die, and it's worse to be dry,
  And I move we pipe to grog.'

"Oh, then 'twas the noble second mate
  What filled them all with awe;
The second mate, as bad men hate,
  And cruel skipper's jaw.

"He took the anchor on his back,
  And leaped into the main;
Through foam and spray he clove his way,
  And sunk and rose again!

"Through foam and spray, a league away
  The anchor stout he bore;
Till, safe at last, he made it fast
  And warped the ship ashore!

" 'Taint much of a job to talk about,
  But a ticklish thing to see,
And suth'in to do, if I say it, too,
  For that second mate was me!"

Such was the tale that was told to me
By that modest and truthful son of the sea,
And I envy the life of a second mate,
Though captains curse him and sailors hate,
For he ain't like some of the swabs I've seen,
As would go and lie to a poor marine.
                              —James Jeffrey Roche.

160

HOMESICK

Last night I heard a sea song,
A wind-is-in-the-lee song,
A where-I-long-to-be song,
   Yo ho, me lads, yo ho!

I saw the black night scowlin'
And heard the wild gales howlin'
Like beasts of prey a-prowlin'—
   It set my heart aglow!

The wind was in the riggin',
The whitecaps were a-jiggin'
And shipmates were a-swiggin'
   Of Java down below.

I saw the palm trees swayin'
And hula maidens playin'
While bosuns' mates were brayin'
   "Get ready for a blow!"

Last night I heard a sea song,
A wind-is-in-the-lee song,
A where-I-long-to-be song,
  On the Radio!
      —*Nick Kenny.*

161

THE LASS THAT LOVED A SAILOR

Once I loved a sailor so dear as my life,
And ofttimes he've told me he would make me his wife;
But now he is gone sick for some other one,
Leaved me and my baby in sorrow to mourn.

O, my parents chastised me, O, because I done so,
But now I am despised by all other ones I know;
My father and mother turned me from the door,
So now I must ramble and beg like one poor.

O, come all ye pretty fair maids, wheresoever ye be,
Don't you trust to any young men by any degree.
They will kiss you and court you and swear they'll prove
    true,
And the very next moment they'll bid you adieu.

162

THE LITTLE SHIPS THAT NEVER SAIL

At work on inland farms he must have dreamed,
In restless youth, of sailing ships that came
With lifted prows where still the wonder gleamed
From seas and ports he loved but could not name.

In him was some old trace of blood that knew
The lift of sails and thrill of blowing spray—
But land had held him and the harvest grew
And he had never dared to go away.

Too old at last for work, his knotted hands
Have turned to dreams his youth saw shining by,
And at a window facing prairie lands
He sees the cloud-ships billowed down the sky.
Each day he sits there, till the light must fail,
To build his little ships that never sail.

—*Glenn Ward Dresbach.*

XI

THE WARRIOR STAG

"And every body praised the Duke
Who this great fight did win."
"But what good came of it at last?"
Quoth little Peterkin:—
"Why that I cannot tell," said he,
But 'twas a famous victory."

—*R. Southey.*

163

THE GLORIES OF OUR BLOOD AND STATE

The glories of our blood and state
  Are shadows, not substantial things;
There is no armour against fate;
  Death lays his icy hand on kings:
    Sceptre and Crown
    Must tumble down,
And in the dust be equal made
With the poor crookèd scythe and spade.

Some men with swords may reap the field,
  And plant fresh laurels where they kill:
But their strong nerves at last must yield;
  They tame but one another still:
    Early or late
    They stoop to fate,
And must give up their murmuring breath,
When they, pale captives, creep to death.

The garlands wither on your brow,
  Then boast no more your mighty deeds;
Upon Death's purple altar now
  See, where the victor-victim bleeds:
    Your heads must come
    To the cold tomb;
Only the actions of the just
Smell sweet, and blossom in their dust.

                —James Shirley.

164

ODE WRITTEN IN MDCCXLVI

How sleep the Brave, who sink to rest
By all their Country's wishes blest!
When Spring, with dewy fingers cold,
Returns to deck their hallow'd mold,
She there shall dress a sweeter sod
Than Fancy's feet have ever trod.

By fairy hands their knell is rung,
By forms unseen their dirge is sung:
There Honor comes, a pilgrim gray,
To bless the turf that wraps their clay;
And Freedom shall awhile repair
To dwell a weeping hermit there!

—*W. Collins.*

165

TO LUCASTA, ON GOING TO THE WARS

Tell me not, Sweet, I am unkind
    That from the nunnery
Of thy chaste breast and quiet mind,
    To war and arms I fly.

True, a new mistress now I chase,
    The first foe in the field;
And with a stronger faith embrace
    A sword, a horse, a shield.

Yet this inconstancy is such
  As you too shall adore;
I could not love thee, Dear, so much,
  Loved I not Honor more.
          —*Colonel Lovelace.*

166

SIR EGLAMOUR

Sir Eglamour, that worthy knight,
He took his sword and went to fight;
And as he rode both hill and dale,
Armed upon his shirt of mail,
A dragon came out of his den,
Had slain, God knows how many men!

When he espied Sir Eglamour,
Oh, if you had but heard him roar,
And seen how all the trees did shake,
The knight did tremble, horse did quake,
The birds betake them all to peeping—
It would have made you fall a weeping!

But now it is in vain to fear,
Being come unto, 'fight dog! fight bear!'
To it they go and fiercely fight.
A live-long day from morn till night.
The dragon had a plaguy hide,
And could the sharpest steel abide.

No sword will enter him with cuts,
Which vexed the knight unto the guts;

But, as in choler he did burn
He watched the dragon a good turn;
And, as a yawning he did fall,
He thrust his sword in hilts and all.

Then, like a coward he to fly
Unto his den that was hard by;
And there he lay all night and roared.
The knight was sorry for his sword
But, riding thence, said, 'I forsake it,
He that will fetch it, let him take it!'

—S. *Rowlands.*

167

I HAVE A RENDEZVOUS WITH DEATH

I have a rendezvous with Death
At some disputed barricade,
When Spring comes back with rustling shade
And apple-blossoms fill the air—
I have a rendezvous with Death
When Spring brings back blue days and fair.

It may be he shall take my hand
And lead me into his dark land
And close my eyes and quench my breath—
It may be I shall pass him still.
I have a rendezvous with Death
On some scarred slope of battered hill
When Spring comes round again this year
And the first meadow-flowers appear.

God knows 'twere better to be deep
Pillowed in silk and scented down,
Where Love throbs out in blissful sleep,
Pulse nigh to pulse, and breath to breath,
Where hushed awakenings are dear . . .
But I've a rendezvous with Death
At midnight in some flaming town,
When Spring trips north again this year,
And I to my pledged word am true,
I shall not fail that rendezvous.

—*Alan Seeger.*

168

THE MAN HE KILLED

"Had he and I but met
By some old ancient inn,
We should have sat us down to wet
Right many a nipperkin!

"But ranged as infantry,
And staring face to face,
I shot at him as he at me,
And killed him in his place.

"I shot him dead because—
Because he was my foe,
Just so: my foe of course he was;
That's clear enough; although

"He thought he'd 'list, perhaps,
Off-hand like—just as I;
Was out of work, had sold his traps—
No other reason why.

"Yes; quaint and curious war is!
You shoot a fellow down
You'd treat if met where any bar is,
Or help to half-a-crown."
　　　　　　—Thomas Hardy.

169

THEY WENT FORTH TO BATTLE, BUT THEY ALWAYS FELL

They went forth to battle, but they always fell;
　　Their eyes were fixed above the sullen shields;
Nobly they fought and bravely, but not well,
And sank heart-wounded by a subtle spell.
　　They knew not fear that to the foeman yields,
　　They were not weak, as one who vainly wields
A futile weapon; yet the sad scrolls tell
How on the hard-fought field they always fell.

It was a secret music that they heard,
　　A sad sweet plea for pity and for peace;
And that which pierced the heart was but a word,
Though the white breast was red-lipped where the
　　　　sword
　　Pressed a fierce cruel kiss, to put surcease
　　On its hot thirst, but drank a hot increase.
Ah, they by some strange troubling doubt were stirred,
And died for hearing what no foeman heard.

They went forth to battle, but they always fell;
　　Their might was not the might of lifted spears;
Over the battle-clamor came a spell
Of troubling music, and they fought not well.

Their wreaths are willows and their tribute, tears;
Their names are old sad stories in men's ears;
Yet they shall scatter the red hordes of Hell,
Who went to battle forth and always fell.

—Shaemas O'Sheel.

XII

THE STAG COURAGEOUS

Though love repine and reason chafe,
There came a voice without reply,—
" 'Tis man's perdition to be safe,
When for the truth he ought to die."

—*Ralph Waldo Emerson.*

170

TO FIGHT ALOUD IS VERY BRAVE

> To fight aloud is very brave,
> But gallanter, I know,
> Who charge within the bosom,
> The cavalry of woe . . .
> —*Emily Dickinson.*

171

GOD, GIVE US MEN!

God, give us men! A time like this demands
  Strong minds, great hearts, true faith and ready
    hands;
  Men whom the lust of office does not kill;
 Men whom the spoils of office can not buy;
  Men who possess opinions and a will;
Men who have honor; men who will not lie;
Men who can stand before a demagogue
  And damn his treacherous flatteries without winking!
Tall men, sun-crowned, who live above the fog
  In public duty, and in private thinking;
For while the rabble, with their thumb-worn creeds,
Their large professions and their little deeds,
Mingle in selfish strife, lo! Freedom weeps,
Wrong rules the land and waiting Justice sleeps.
                    —*Josiah Gilbert Holland.*

172

FREEDOM

. . .

We are not free: Freedom doth not consist
In musing with our faces toward the Past,
While petty cares, and crawling interests, twist
Their spider-threads about us, which at last
Grow strong as iron chains, to cramp and bind
In formal narrowness heart, soul, and mind.
Freedom is recreated year by year,
In hearts wide open on the Godward side,
In souls calm-cadenced as the whirling sphere,
In minds that sway the future like a tide.
No broadest creeds can hold her, and no codes;
She chooses men for her august abodes,
Building them fair and fronting to the dawn;
Yet, when we seek her, we but find a few
Light footprints, leading morn-ward through the dew;
Before the day had risen, she was gone.

And we must follow: swiftly runs she on,
And, if our steps should slacken in despair,
Half turns her face, half smiles, through golden hair,
Forever yielding, never wholly won:
That is not love which pauses in the race
Two close-linked names on fleeting sand to trace;
Freedom gained yesterday is no more ours;
Men gather but dry seeds of last year's flowers;
Still there's a charm ungranted, still a grace,
Still rosy Hope, the free, the unattained,
Makes us Possession's languid hand let fall;

'Tis but a fragment of ourselves is gained,—
The Future brings us more, but never all.

. . .

—*James Russell Lowell.*

173

COLUMBUS

Behind him lay the gray Azores,
Behind the Gates of Hercules;
Before him not the ghost of shores:
Before him only shoreless seas.
The good mate said: "Now must we pray,
For lo! the very stars are gone.
Brave Adm'r'l, speak; what shall I say?"
"Why, say: 'Sail on! sail on! and on!'"

"My men grow mutinous day by day;
My men grow ghastly wan and weak."
The stout mate thought of home; a spray
Of salt wave washed his swarthy cheek.
"What shall I say, brave Adm'r'l, say,
If we sight naught but seas at dawn?"
"Why, you shall say at break of day:
'Sail on! sail on! sail on! and on!'"

They sailed and sailed, as winds might blow,
Until at last the blanched mate said:
"Why, now not even God would know
Should I and all my men fall dead.
These very winds forget their way,
For God from these dread seas is gone.
Now speak, brave Adm'r'l; speak and say—
He said: "Sail on! sail on! and on!"

They sailed. They sailed. Then spake the mate:
"This mad sea shows his teeth to-night.
He curls his lip, he lies in wait,
With lifted teeth, as if to bite!
Brave Adm'r'l, say but one good word:
What shall we do when hope is gone?"
The words leapt like a leaping sword:
"Sail on! sail on! sail on! and on!"

Then, pale and worn, he kept his deck,
And peered through darkness. Ah, that night
Of all dark nights! And then a speck—
A light! A light! A light! A light!
It grew, a starlit flag unfurled!
It grew to be Time's burst of dawn.
He gained a world; he gave that world
Its grandest lesson: "On! sail on!"

—*Joaquin Miller.*

174

MACPHERSON'S FAREWELL

Farewell, ye dungeons dark and strong,
The wretche's destinie!
Macpherson's time will not be long
On yonder gallows-tree.
  Sae rantingly, sae wantonly,
  Sae dauntingly gaed he;
  He played a spring, and danced it round
  Below the gallows-tree.

Oh, what is death but parting breath?
On many a bloody plain

I've dared his face, and in this place
I scorn him yet again!

Untie these bands from off my hands,
And bring to me my sword;
And there's no man in all Scotland
But I'll brave him at a word.

I've lived a life of sturt and strife;
I die by treacherie:
It burns my heart I must depart,
And not avenged be.

Now farewell light, thou sunshine bright,
And all beneath the sky!
May coward shame distain his name,
The wretch that dares not die!

—*Robert Burns.*

175

REFLECTIONS

I saw a man
With drooping shoulders,
His clothes disarrayed
And in his eyes
A haunting look
Of sadness.
And by these signs
I knew his heart
Was breaking
For he was just
Like other men
Who risk
Their peace of mind
And lose
In some sweet
Enterprise.

And so I thought
If he had
Owned a heart
Of flint that flashes
Fire
But softens not
I would not see
Him
Broken now

With sorrow.
But then I knew
A heart like that
Could never
Know the sweet
Details of tasted
Joys
He must have known
To be so
Brokenhearted.

And so perhaps
He would
Prefer to have it
Thus,
To live with such
Intensity
That every day
His heart would know

The breathlessness
Of Joy
Or the depths
Of uttermost
Depression.

And realizing this
I smiled
At him
For smiles are said
To help a fellow
On his way
And he smiled
Back at me
For it was I
Standing there
Smiling back at me
Through
The looking-glass.

—*Dudley C. Phillips.*

176

TO-DAY

Sure, this world is full of trouble—
　　I ain't said it ain't.
Lord! I've had enough, an' double,
　　Reason for complaint.
Rain an' storm have come to fret me,
　　Skies were often gray;
Thorns an' brambles have beset me
　　On the road—but, say,
　　Ain't it fine to-day?

What's the use of always weepin',
　　Makin' trouble last?
What's the use of always keepin'
　　Thinkin' of the past?
Each must have his tribulation,
　　Water with his wine.
Life it ain't no celebration.
　　Trouble? I've had mine—
　　But to-day is fine.

It's to-day that I am livin',
　　Not a month ago,
Havin', losin', takin', givin',
　　As time wills it so.
Yesterday a cloud of sorrow
　　Fell across the way;
It may rain again to-morrow,
　　It may rain—but, say,
　　Ain't it fine to-day!
　　　　　—Douglas Malloch.

177

IT COULDN'T BE DONE

Somebody said that it couldn't be done,
　　But he with a chuckle replied
That "maybe it couldn't," but he would be one
　　Who wouldn't say so till he'd tried.
So he buckled right in with the trace of a grin
　　On his face. If he worried he hid it.
He started to sing as he tackled the thing
　　That couldn't be done, and he did it.

Somebody scoffed: "Oh, you'll never do that;
    At least no one ever has done it";
But he took off his coat and he took off his hat,
    And the first thing we knew he'd begun it.
With a lift of his chin and a bit of a grin,
    Without any doubting or quiddit,
He started to sing as he tackled the thing
    That couldn't be done, and he did it.

There are thousands to tell you it cannot be done,
    There are thousands to prophesy failure;
There are thousands to point out to you one by one,
    The dangers that wait to assail you.
But just buckle in with a bit of a grin,
    Just take off your coat and go to it;
Just start to sing as you tackle the thing
    That "cannot be done," and you'll do it.
                              —*Edgar A. Guest.*

178

COURAGE AND ONWARD

Some folks that strive get all the breaks
While others strive and get heartaches.
If you are in the latter class
Don't groan "Some day this, too, will pass."
Just buckle down for all you're worth
For there's no waste on this old earth.
I've pondered long and it is clear
There's some good reason why we're here.
Tears won't help so no use crying;
Time is better spent in trying;
Lift up your thought, and then your feet

Will go a-prancing up the street,
Throw out your chin and see it through
'Cause, man, there's nothing else to do!
                                        —*Ona Cragg.*

179

DIAGNOSIS

It's a bitter old world, is it not?
    It's a dreary old place—am I right?
It's a dirty old deal? Oh, I know how you feel—
    You are in such a terrible plight!
But the sky—well, it seems to be blue,
    And there's music enough in the trees,
And the sun's shining bright, and the earth is all right—
    So I wouldn't blame it on these.

It's a rugged old road at the best?
    Sure, I know. And you're sick of the gloom?
But there's nothing much wrong with the bob-o-link's
        song
    Or the way that the daffodils bloom.
Why, the bluebirds are cheering you on!
    And the ground's even soft where you fall!
Not a thing's out of whack on the little old track—
    So maybe it's you, after all.

                                        —*Larry Flint.*

180

DON'T QUIT

When things go wrong as they sometimes will,
When the road you're trudging seems all uphill,

When the funds are low and the debts are high
And you want to smile, but have to sigh,
When care is pressing you down a bit,
Rest, if you must, but don't you quit.
Life is queer with its twists and turns,
As everyone of us sometimes learns,
And many a failure turns about
When he might have won had he stuck it out:

Don't give up though the pace seems slow—
You may succeed with another blow.
Success is failure turned inside out—
The silver tint of the clouds of doubt,
And you never can tell how close you are,
It may be near when it seems far:

So stick to the fight when you're hardest hit—
It's when things seem worst that you must not quit.
                                        —*Anonymous.*

181

KEEP ON KEEPIN' ON

If the day looks kinder gloomy
And your chances kinder slim,
If the situation's puzzlin'
And the prospect's awful grim,
If perplexities keep pressin'
Till hope is nearly gone,
Just bristle up and grit your teeth
And keep on keepin' on.

Frettin' never wins a fight
And fumin' never pays;

There ain't no use in broodin'
In these pessimistic ways;
Smile just kinder cheerfully
Though hope is nearly gone,
And bristle up and grit your teeth
And keep on keepin' on.

There ain't no use in growlin'
And grumblin' all the time,
When music's ringin' everywhere
And everything's a rhyme.
Just keep on smilin' cheerfully
If hope is nearly gone,
And bristle up and grit your teeth
And keep on keepin' on.

—*Anonymous.*

182

AN UPHILL FIGHT

You may be ill and you may be sore
With aches and bruises and pains galore;
Perhaps you are groggy, and halt and lame,
But keep right on, for it's all a game
Where like as not you are booked to win
Right now, in spite of the shape you're in.

Your brain is weary, your thoughts are dead
Each step is heavy as lifting lead;
The sun is passing under a cloud;
Don't let them measure you for a shroud,
But hang on now though it may be hard,
For your next hand holds the winning card.

If you have played at a losing game
Until the colors all look the same,
You'll feel more joy when your luck has turned,
And look on life, which you may have spurned,
Through eyes that glow with the glory light
That comes from winning an uphill fight.

—*Maurice Waugh.*

183

A POOR UNFORTUNATE

I

His hoss went dead an' his mule went lame;
He lost six cows in a poker game;
A harricane came on a summer's day,
An' carried the house whar' he lived away;
Then a airthquake come when they wuz gone,
An' swallered the lan' that the house stood on!
An' the tax collector, *he* come roun'
An' charged him up fer the hole in the groun'!
An' the city marshal—he come in view
An' said he wanted his street tax, too!

II

Did he moan an' sigh? Did he set an' cry
An' cuss the harricane sweepin' by?
Did he grieve that his ol' friends failed to call
When the airthquake come an' swallered all?
Never a word o' blame he said,
With all them troubles on top his head!
Not him. . . . He clumb to the top o' the hill—
Whar' standin' room wuz left him still,

An', barin' his head, here's what he said:
"I reckon it's time to git up an' git;
But, Lord, I hain't had the measles yit!"
—*Frank L. Stanton.*

184

THE FIGHTER

I fight a battle every day
  Against discouragement and fear;
Some foe stands always in my way,
  The path ahead is never clear!
I must forever be on guard
  Against the doubts that skulk along;
I get ahead by fighting hard,
  But fighting keeps my spirit strong.

I hear the croakings of Despair,
  The dark predictions of the weak;
I find myself pursued by Care,
  No matter what the end I seek;
My victories are small and few,
  It matters not how hard I strive;
Each day the fight begins anew,
  But fighting keeps my hopes alive.

My dreams are spoiled by circumstance,
  My plans are wrecked by Fate or Luck;
Some hour, perhaps, will bring my chance,
  But that great hour has never struck;
My progress has been slow and hard,
  I've had to climb and crawl and swim,
Fighting for every stubborn yard,
  But I have kept in fighting trim.

I have to fight my doubts away,
  And be on guard against my fears;
The feeble croaking of Dismay
  Has been familiar through the years;
My dearest plans keep going wrong,
  Events combine to thwart my will,
But fighting keeps my spirit strong,
  And I am undefeated still!

—*S. E. Kiser.*

185

LIFE AND DEATH

So he died for his faith. That is fine—
  More than most of us do.
But stay, can you add to that line
  That he lived for it, too?

In death he bore witness at last
  As a martyr to truth.
Did his life do the same in the past
  From the days of his youth?

It is easy to die. Men have died
  For a wish or a whim—
From bravado or passion or pride.
  Was it harder for him?

But to live: every day to live out
  All the truth that he dreamt,
While his friends met his conduct with doubt,
  And the world with contempt—

Was it thus that he plodded ahead,
  Never turning aside?
Then we'll talk of the life that he led—
  Never mind how he died.

—Ernest H. Crosby.

186

HOW DID YOU DIE?

Did you tackle that trouble that came your way
  With a resolute heart and cheerful?
Or hide your face from the light of day
  With a craven soul and fearful?
Oh, a trouble's a ton, or a trouble's an ounce,
  Or a trouble is what you make it,
And it isn't the fact that you're hurt that counts,
  But only how did you take it?

You are beaten to earth? Well, well, what's that!
  Come up with a smiling face.
It's nothing against you to fall down flat,
  But to lie there—that's disgrace.
The harder you're thrown, why the higher you bounce
  Be proud of your blackened eye!
It isn't the fact that you're licked that counts;
  It's how did you fight—and why?

And though you be done to the death, what then?
  If you battled the best you could,
If you played your part in the world of men,
  Why, the Critic will call it good.

Death comes with a crawl, or comes with a pounce,
   And whether he's slow or spry,
It isn't the fact that you're dead that counts,
   But only how did you die?

                   —*Edmund Vance Cooke.*

187

TO THE MEN WHO LOSE

   Here's to the men who lose!
What though their work be e'er so nobly planned,
   And watched with zealous care,
No glorious halo crowns their efforts grand,
   Contempt is failure's share.

   Here's to the men who lose!
If triumph's easy smile our struggles greet,
   Courage is easy then;
The king is he who, after fierce defeat,
   Can up and fight again.

   Here's to the men who lose!
The ready plaudits of a fawning world
   Ring sweet in victor's ears;
The vanquished's banners never are unfurled—
   For them there sound no cheers.

   Here's to the men who lose!
The touchstone of true worth is not success;
   There is a higher test—
Though fate may darkly frown, onward to press,
   And bravely do one's best.

Here's to the men who lose!
It is the vanquished's praises that I sing,
   And this is the toast I choose;
"A hard-fought failure is a noble thing;
   Here's to the men who lose!"

                         —Anonymous.

XIII

CABBAGES AND KINGS

"The time has come" the Walrus said
    "To speak of many things—
Of shoes, and ships, and sealing-wax
    And cabbages and kings."

—*Lewis Carroll.*

188

THE SLAVE

They set the slave free, striking off his chains . . .
Then he was as much of a slave as ever.

He was still chained to servility,
He was still manacled to indolence and sloth,
He was still bound by fear and superstition,
By ignorance, suspicion, and savagery . . .
His slavery was not in the chains,
But in himself . . .

They can only set free men free . . .
And there is no need of that:
Free men set themselves free.

—*James Oppenheim.*

189

THE HIGHWAYMAN

Part One

I

The wind was a torrent of darkness among the gusty trees,
The moon was a ghostly galleon tossed upon cloudy seas,
The road was a ribbon of moonlight over the purple moor,
And the highwayman came riding—
    Riding—riding—
The highwayman came riding, up to the old inn-door.

II

He'd a French cocked-hat on his forehead, a bunch of lace
  at his chin,
A coat of the claret velvet, and breeches of brown doeskin:
They fitted with never a wrinkle; his boots were up to the
  thigh!
And he rode with a jewelled twinkle,
     His pistol butts a-twinkle,
His rapier hilt a-twinkle, under the jewelled sky.

III

Over the cobbles he clattered and clashed in the dark inn-
  yard,
And he tapped with his whip on the shutters, but all was
  locked and barred:
He whistled a tune to the window, and who should be wait-
  ing there
But the landlord's black-eyed daughter,
     Bess, the landlord's daughter,
Plaiting a dark red love-knot into her long black hair.

IV

And dark in the dark old inn-yard a stable-wicket creaked
Where Tim, the 'ostler, listened; his face was white and
  peaked,
His eyes were hollows of madness, his hair like moldy hay;
But he loved the landlord's daughter,
     The landlord's red-lipped daughter:
Dumb as a dog he listened, and he heard the robber say—

V

"One kiss, my bonny sweetheart, I'm after a prize tonight,
But I shall be back with the yellow gold before the morning
  light.

Yet if th⌄y press me sharply, and harry me through the day,
Then look for me by moonlight,
    Watch for me by moonlight:
I'll come to thee by moonlight, though Hell should bar
the way."

VI

He rose upright in the stirrups, he scarce could reach her
hand;
But she loosened her hair i' the casement! His face burnt
like a brand
As the black cascade of perfume came tumbling over his
breast;
And he kissed its waves in the moonlight,
    (Oh, sweet black waves in the moonlight)
Then he tugged at his reins in the moonlight, and galloped
away to the West.

Part Two
I

He did not come in the dawning; he did not come at noon;
And out of the tawny sunset, before the rise o' the moon,
When the road was a gypsy's ribbon, looping the purple
moor,
A red-coat troop came marching—
    Marching—marching—
King George's men came marching, up to the old inn-door.

II

They said no word to the landlord, they drank his ale instead;
But they gagged his daughter and bound her to the foot of
her narrow bed.

Two of them knelt at her casement, with muskets at the side!
There was death at every window;
    And Hell at one dark window;
For Bess could see, through her casement, the road that *he*
    would ride.

III

They had tied her up to attention, with many a sniggering
    jest:
They had bound a musket beside her, with the barrel be-
    neath her breast!
"Now keep good watch!" and they kissed her.
    She heard the dead man say—
Look for me by moonlight;
    Watch for me by moonlight;
I'll come to thee by moonlight, though Hell should bar the
    way!

IV

She twisted her hands behind her; but all the knots held
    good!
She writhed her hands till her fingers were wet with sweat
    or blood!
They stretched and strained in the darkness, and the hours
    crawled by like years;
Till, now, on the stroke of midnight,
    Cold, on the stroke of midnight,
The tip of one finger touched it! The trigger at least was
    hers!

V

The tip of one finger touched it; she strove no more for the
    rest!

Up, she stood to attention, with the barrel beneath her breast,
She would not risk their hearing: she would not strive again;
For the road lay bare in the moonlight,
    Blank and bare in the moonlight;
And the blood of her veins in the moonlight throbbed to her
    Love's refrain.

VI

Tlot-tlot; tlot-tlot! Had they heard it? The horse-hoofs ring-
    ing clear—
Tlot-tlot, tlot-tlot in the distance? Were they deaf that they
    did not hear?
Down the ribbon of moonlight, over the brow of the hill,
The highwayman came riding,
    Riding, riding!   .
The red-coats looked to their priming! She stood up straight
    and still!

VII

Tlot-tlot, in the frosty silence! *Tlot-tlot* in the echoing night!
Nearer he came and nearer! Her face was like a light!
Her eyes grew wide for a moment; she drew one last deep
    breath,
Then her finger moved in the moonlight,
    Her musket shattered the moonlight,
Shattered her breast in the moonlight and warned him—with
    her death.

VIII

He turned; he spurred him Westward; he did not know who
    stood
Bowed with her head o'er the musket, drenched with her
    own red blood!

Not till the dawn he heard it, and slowly blanched to hear
How Bess, the landlord's daughter,
    The landlord's black-eyed daughter,
Had watched for her Love in the moonlight, and died in the
    darkness there.

IX

Back, he spurred like a madman, shrieking a curse to the sky,
With the white road smoking behind him, and his rapier
    brandished high!
Blood-red were his spurs i' the golden noon; wine-red was
    his velvet coat;
When they shot him down on the highway,
    Down like a dog on the highway,
And he lay in his blood on the highway, with the bunch of
    lace at his throat.

       .   .   .

*And still of a winter's night, they say, when the wind is in
    the trees,*
When the moon is a ghostly galleon tossed upon cloudy seas,
*When the road is a ribbon of moonlight over the purple
    moor,*
A highwayman comes riding—
    Riding—riding—
A highwayman comes riding, up to the old inn-door.

X

Over the cobbles he clatters and clangs in the dark inn-yard;
*And he taps with his whip on the shutters, but all is locked
    and barred:*
*He whistles a tune to the window, and who should be wait-
    ing there*

But the landlord's black-eyed daughter,
*   Bess, the landlord's daughter,*
Plaiting a dark red love-knot into her long black hair.
                                        —*Alfred Noyes.*

190

A BALLAD OF A NUN

From Eastertide to Eastertide
    For ten long years her patient knees
Engraved the stones—the fittest bride
    Of Christ in all the diocese.

She conquered every earthly lust;
    The abbess loved her more and more;
And, as a mark of perfect trust,
    Made her the keeper of the door.

High on a hill the convent hung,
    Across a duchy looking down,
Where everlasting mountains flung
    Their shadows over tower and town.

The hewels of their lofty snows
    In constellations flashed at night;
Above their crests the moon arose;
    The deep earth shuddered with delight.

Long ere she left her cloudy bed,
    Still dreaming in the orient land,
On many a mountain's happy head
    Dawn lightly laid her rosy hand.

The adventurous sun took Heaven by storm;
  Clouds scattered largesses of rain;
The sounding cities, rich and warm,
  Smouldered and glittered in the plain.

Sometimes it was a wandering wind,
  Sometimes the fragrance of the pine,
Sometimes the thought how others sinned,
  That turned her sweet blood into wine.

Sometimes she heard a serenade
  Complaining sweetly far away:
She said, "A young man woos a maid";
  And dreamt of love till break of day.

Then would she ply her knotted scourge
  Until she swooned; but evermore
She had the same red sin to purge,
  Poor, passionate keeper of the door!

For still night's starry scroll unfurled,
  And still the day came like a flood:
It was the greatness of the world
  That made her long to use her blood.

In winter-time when Lent drew nigh,
  And hill and plain were wrapped in snow,
She watched beneath the frosty sky
  The nearest city nightly glow.

Like peals of airy bells outworn,
  Faint laughter died above her head
In gusts of broken music borne:
  "They keep the Carnival," she said.

Her hungry heart devoured the town:
  "Heaven save me by a miracle!
Unless God sends an angel down,
  Thither I go though it were Hell."

She dug her nails deep in her breast,
  Sobbed, shrieked, and straight withdrew the bar:
A fledgling flying from the nest,
  A pale moth rushing to a star.

Fillet and veil in strips she tore;
  Her golden tresses floated wide;
The ring and bracelet that she wore
  As Christ's betrothed, she cast aside.

"Life's dearest meaning I shall probe;
  Lo! I shall taste of love at last!
Away!" She doffed her outer robe,
  And sent it sailing down the blast.

Her body seemed to warm the wind;
  With bleeding feet o'er ice she ran:
"I leave the righteous God behind;
  I go to worship sinful man."

She reached the sounding city's gate;
  No question did the warder ask:
He passed her in: "Welcome, wild mate!"
  He thought her some fantastic mask.

Half-naked through the town she went;
  Each footstep left a bloody mark;
Crowds followed her with looks intent;
  Her bright eyes made the torches dark.

Alone and watching in the street
   There stood a grave youth nobly dressed;
To him she knelt and kissed his feet;
   Her face her great desire confessed.

Straight to his house the nun he led:
   "Strange lady, what would you of me?"
"Your love, your love, sweet lord," she said;
   "I bring you my virginity."

He healed her bosom with a kiss;
   She gave him all her passion's hoard;
And sobbed and murmured ever, "This
   Is life's great meaning, dear, my lord.

"I care not for my broken vow;
   Though God should come in thunder soon,
I am sister to the mountains now,
   And sister to the sun and moon."

Through all the towns of Belmarie
   She made a progress like a queen.
"She is," they said, "whate'er she be,
   The strangest woman ever seen.

"From fairyland she must have come,
   Or else she is a mermaiden."
Some said she was a ghoul, and some
   A heathen goddess born again.

But soon her fire to ashes burned;
   Her beauty changed to haggardness;
Her golden hair to silver turned;
   The hour came of her last caress.

At midnight from her lonely bed
   She rose, and said, "I have had my will."
The ragged robe she donned, and fled
   Back to the convent on the hill.

Half-naked as she went before,
   She hurried to the city wall,
Unnoticed in the rush and roar
   And splendour of the Carnival.

No question did the warder ask:
   Her ragged robe, her shrunken limb,
Her dreadful eyes! "It is no mask;
   It is a she-wolf, gaunt and grim!"

She ran across the icy plain;
   Her worn blood curdled in the blast;
Each footstep left a crimson stain;
   The white-faced moon looked on aghast.

She said between her chattering jaws,
   "Deep peace is mine, I cease to strive;
Oh, comfortable convent laws,
   That bury foolish nuns alive!

"A trowel for my passing-bell,
   A little bed within the wall,
A coverlet of stones; how well
   I there shall keep the Carnival!"

Like tired bells chiming in their sleep,
   The wind faint peals of laughter bore;
She stopped her ears and climbed the steep,
   And thundered at the convent door.

It opened straight; she entered in,
  And at the wardress' feet fell prone:
"I come to purge away my sin;
  Bury me, close me up in stone."

The wardress raised her tenderly;
  She touched her wet and fast-shut eyes:
"Look, sister; sister, look at me;
  Look; can you see through my disguise?"

She looked and saw her own sad face,
  And trembled, wondering, "Who art thou?"
"God sent me down to fill your place:
  I am the Virgin Mary now."

And with the word, God's mother shone:
  The wanderer whispered, "Mary, hail!"
The vision helped her to put on
  Bracelet and fillet, ring and veil.

"You are sister to the mountains now,
  And sister to the day and night;
Sister to God." And on the brow
  She kissed her thrice, and left her sight.

While dreaming in her cloudy bed,
  Far in the crimson orient land,
On many a mountain's happy head
  Dawn lightly laid her rosy head.
                              —*John Davidson.*

191

EACH IN HIS OWN TONGUE

A Fire-Mist and a planet,—
   A crystal and a cell,—
A jelly-fish and a saurian,
   And caves where the cave-men dwell;
Then a sense of law and beauty,
   And a face turned from the clod,—
Some call it Evolution,
   And others call it God.

A haze on the far horizon,
   The infinite, tender sky,
The ripe, rich tint of the cornfields,
   And the wild geese sailing high,—
And all over upland and lowland
   The charm of the goldenrod,—
Some of us call it Autumn,
   And others call it God.

Like tides on a crescent sea-beach,
   When the moon is new and thin,
Into our hearts high yearnings
   Come welling and surging in,—
Come from the mystic ocean
   Whose rim no foot has trod,—
Some of us call it Longing,
   And others call it God.

A picket frozen on duty,—
   A mother starved for her brood,—
Socrates drinking the hemlock,
   And Jesus on the rood;

And millions who, humble and nameless,
   The straight, hard pathway plod,—
Some call it Consecration,
   And others call it God.
          —*William Herbert Carruth.*

192

RUBÁIYÁT OF OMAR KHÁYYAM

Come, fill the Cup, and in the fire of Spring
Your Winter-garment of Repentance fling:
   The Bird of Time has but a little way
To flutter—and the Bird is on the Wing.

Whether at Naishápúr or Babylon,
Whether the Cup with sweet or bitter run,
   The Wine of Life keeps oozing drop by drop,
The Leaves of Life keep falling one by one.

A Book of Verses underneath the Bough,
A Jug of Wine, a Loaf of Bread—and Thou
   Beside me singing in the Wilderness—
Oh, Wilderness were Paradise enow!

Some for the Glories of this World; and some
Sigh for the Prophet's Paradise to come;
   Ah, take the Cash, and let the Credit go,
Nor heed the rumble of a distant Drum!

The Worldly Hope men set their Hearts upon
Turns Ashes—or it prospers; and anon,
   Like Snow upon the Desert's dusty Face,
Lighting a little hour or two—is gone.

Think, in this battered caravanserai
Whose portals are alternate Night and Day,
  How Sultán after Sultán with his Pomp
Abode his destined Hour, and went his way.

I sometimes think that never blows so red
The Rose as where some buried Caesar bled;
  That every Hyacinth the Garden wears
Dropped in her lap from some once lovely Head.

And this reviving Herb whose tender Green
Fledges the River-Lip on which we lean—
  Ah, lean upon it lightly! for who knows
From what once lovely Lip it springs unseen!

Ah, my Beloved, fill the Cup that clears
TO-DAY of past Regret and future Fears:
  TO-MORROW!—Why, To-morrow I may be
Myself with Yesterday's Seven thousand Years.

For some we loved, the loveliest and the best
That from his Vintage rolling Time hath pressed,
  Have drunk their Cup a Round or two before,
And one by one crept silently to rest.

And we that now make merry in the Room
They left, and Summer dresses in new bloom,
  Ourselves must we beneath the Couch of Earth
Descend—ourselves to make a Couch—for whom?

Ah, make the most of what we yet may spend,
Before we too into the Dust descend;
  Dust into Dust, and under Dust, to lie,
Sans Wine, sans Song, sans Singer, and—sans End!

Myself when young did eagerly frequent
Doctor and Saint, and heard great argument
    About it and about: but evermore
Came out by the same door where in I went.

With them the seed of Wisdom did I sow,
And with mine own hand wrought to make it grow;
    And this was all the Harvest that I reaped—
"I came like Water, and like Wind I go."

Up from the Earth's Center through the Seventh Gate
I rose, and on the Throne of Saturn sage,
    And many a knot unravelled by the Road;
But not the Master-knot of Human Fate.

There was the Door to which I found no Key;
There was the Veil through which I might not see,
    Some little talk awhile of *Me* and *Thee*
There was—and then no more of *Thee* and *Me*.

Strange, is it not? that of the myriads who
Before us passed the door of darkness through,
    No one returns to tell us of the Road,
Which to discover we must travel too.

The Revelations of Devout and Learned
Who rose before us, and as Prophets burned,
    Are all but Stories, which, awoke from Sleep,
They told their comrades and to sleep returned.

I sent my Soul through the Invisible
Some letter of that After-life to spell;
    And by and by my Soul returned to me,
And answered, "I Myself am Heaven and Hell."

Heaven but the Vision of fulfilled Desire,
And Hell the Shadow from a Soul on fire
   Cast on the Darkness into which Ourselves
So late emerged from, shall so soon expire.

We are no other than a moving row
Of magic Shadow-shapes that come and go
   Round with the Sun-illumined Lantern held
In Midnight by the Master of the Show;

But helpless Pieces of the Game He plays
Upon this Checker-board of Nights and Days;
   Hither and thither moves, and checks, and slays,
And one by one back in the Closet lays.

The Ball no question makes of Ayes and Noes,
But Here or There, as strikes the Player, goes;
   And He that tossed you down into the Field,
He knows about it all—HE knows—HE knows!

The Moving Finger writes; and, having writ,
Moves on: nor all your Piety nor Wit
   Shall lure it back to cancel half a Line
Nor all your Tears wash out a Word of it.

And that inverted Bowl they call the Sky,
Whereunder crawling cooped we live and die,
   Lift not your hands to *It* for help—for it
As impotently moves as you or I.

O Thou, who Man of Baser Earth didst make,
And even with Paradise devise the Snake:
   For all the Sin wherewith the Face of Man
Is blackened—Man's forgiveness give—and take!

     ❋   ❋   ❋

As under cover of departing Day
Slunk hunger-stricken Ramazán away,
    Once more within the Potter's house alone
I stood surrounded by the Shapes of Clay.

Shapes of all Sorts and Sizes, great and small,
That stood along the floor and by the wall;
    And some loquacious vessels were; and some
Listened perhaps, but never talked at all.

Said one among them—"Surely not in vain
My substance of the common Earth was ta'en
    And to this Figure molded, to be broke,
Or trampled back to shapeless Earth again."

After a momentary silence spake
Some Vessel of a more ungainly make:
    "They sneer at me for leaning all awry:
What! did the Hand then of the Potter shake?"

So while the Vessels one by one were speaking,
The little Moon looked in that all were seeking:
    And then they jogged each other, "Brother! Brother!
Now for the Porter's shoulder-knot a-creaking!"

Ah, with the Grape my fading Life provide,
And wash the Body whence the Life has died,
    And lay me, shrouded in the living Leaf,
By some not unfrequented Garden-side.

                                —*Edward Fitzgerald.*

193

WAITING

Serene, I fold my hands and wait,
   Nor care for wind, or tide, or sea;
I rave no more 'gainst Time or Fate,
   For, lo! my own shall come to me.

I stay my haste, I make delays,
   For what avails this eager pace?
I stand amid the eternal ways,
   And what is mine shall know my face.

Asleep, awake, by night or day,
   The friends I seek are seeking me;
No wind can drive my bark astray,
   Nor change the tide of destiny.

What matter if I stand alone?
   I wait with joy the coming years;
My heart shall reap where it hath sown,
   And garner up its fruits of tears.

The waters know their own and draw
   The brook that springs in yonder heights;
So flows the good with equal law
   Unto the soul of pure delights.

The stars come nightly to the sky;
   The tidal wave comes to the sea;
Nor time, nor space, nor deep, nor high,
   Can keep my own away from me.
                              —*John Burroughs.*

194

INVICTUS

Out of the night that covers me,
 Black as the Pit from pole to pole,
I thank whatever gods may be
 For my unconquerable soul.

In the fell clutch of circumstance
 I have not winced nor cried aloud.
Under the bludgeonings of chance
 My head is bloody, but unbowed.

Beyond this place of wrath and tears
 Looms but the Horror of the shade,
And yet the menace of the years
 Finds and shall find me unafraid.

It matters not how strait the gate,
 How charged with punishments the scroll,
I am the master of my fate:
 I am the captain of my soul.
 —*William Ernest Henley.*

195

THE BALLAD OF READING GAOL

. . .

Yet each man kills the thing he loves,
 By each let this be heard,
Some do it with a bitter look,

Some with a flattering word,
The coward does it with a kiss,
    The brave man with a sword!

Some kill their love when they are young,
    And some when they are old;
Some strangle with the hands of Lust,
    Some with the hands of Gold:
The kindest use a knife, because
    The dead so soon grow cold.

Some love too little, some too long,
    Some sell, and others buy;
Some do the deed with many tears,
    And some without a sigh:
For each man kills the thing he loves,
    Yet each man does not die. . . .

                    ·   ·   ·

                            —*Oscar Wilde.*

196

DUTY

When Duty comes a-knocking at your gate,
Welcome him in, for if you bid him wait,
He will depart only to come once more
And bring seven other duties to your door.
                            —*Edwin Markham.*

197

SPRING SONG

.   .   .

Only make me over, April,
When the sap begins to stir!
Make me man or make me woman,
Make me oaf or ape or human,
Cup of flower or cone of fir;
Make me anything but neuter
When the sap begins to stir!

—*Bliss Carman.*

XIV

THE STAG SUPPLIANT

Great God, I ask for no meaner pelf
Than that I may not disappoint myself;
That in my action I may soar as high
As I can now discern with this clear eye.

—*Henry David Thoreau.*

198

I know You're the God of the wise and the good—
  Men say You're the God of the strong;
But I hope You're the God of us blundering fools
  Who have faltered and stumbled along!

The wise need so little, the good are all blest;
  Their strength for the strong You renew.
Oh, I hope You find time, in Your infinite plan—
  For we weak ones have nothing but You!
                    —*Roscoe Gilmore Stott.*

199

DISCIPLINE

Throw away Thy rod,
Throw away Thy wrath;
  O my God,
Take the gentle path!

For my heart's desire
Unto Thine is bent:
  I aspire
To a full consent.

Not a work or look
I affect to own,
  But by book,
And Thy Book alone.

Though I fail, I weep;
Though I halt in pace,
  Yet I creep
To the throne of grace.

.   .   .

Throw away Thy rod;
Though man frailties hath,
  Thou art God:
Throw away Thy wrath!
    —*George Herbert.*

200
A HYMN

O God of earth and altar,
  Bow down and hear our cry,
Our earthly rulers falter,
  Our people drift and die;
The walls of gold entomb us,
  The swords of scorn divide,
Take not thy thunder from us,
  But take away our pride.

From all that terror teaches,
  From lies of tongue and pen,
From all the easy speeches
  That comfort cruel men,
From sale and profanation
  Of honour and the sword,
From sleep and from damnation,
  Deliver us, good Lord!

Tie in a living tether
  The prince and priest and thrall,
Bind all our lives together,
  Smite us and save us all;
In ire and exultation
  Aflame with faith, and free,
Lift up a living nation,
  A single sword to thee.
    —*Gilbert Keith Chesterton.*

201

CALIBAN IN THE COAL MINES

God, we don't like to complain—
  We know that the mine is no lark—
But—there's the pools from the rain;
  But—there's the cold and the dark.

God, You don't know what it is—
  You, in Your well-lighted sky,
Watching the meteors whizz;
  Warm, with the sun always by.

God, if You had but the moon
  Stuck in Your cap for a lamp,
Even You'd tire of it soon,
  Down in the dark and the damp.

Nothing but blackness above,
  And nothing that moves but the cars—
God, if You wish for our love,
  Fling us a handful of stars!
    —*Louis Untermeyer.*

202

PRAYERS OF STEEL

Lay me on an anvil, O God.
Beat me and hammer me into a crowbar.
Let me pry loose old walls;
Let me lift and loosen old foundations.

Lay me on an anvil, O God.
Beat me and hammer me into a steel spike.
Drive me into the girders that hold a skyscraper together.
Take red-hot rivets and fasten me into the central girders.
Let me be the great nail holding a skyscraper through blue
    nights into white stars.

—*Carl Sandburg.*

203

CRAFTSMAN

Since I was a lad
Living home with my dad
A feeling I've had
That is good:
That some day I'd find
A real peace of mind,
And make something good
Out of wood.

This job is okay
And besides it's good pay,
But I'd leave it today
If I could,

Just to go out somewhere
And breathe God's pure air,
And make something good
Out of wood.

Alas, when I die
And go up to the sky,
And I will if I try—
And I should—
I'll fall on my knees
And say, Lord, if you please,
Let me make something good
Out of wood.

—Harry K. Glanding.

204
BLESSING ON LITTLE BOYS

God bless all little boys who look like Puck,
　With wide eyes, wider mouths and stick-out ears,
Rash little boys who stay alive by luck
　And Heaven's favor in this world of tears,
Ten-thousand-question-asking little boys,
　Rapid of hand and foot and thought as well,
Playing with gorgeous fancies more than toys,
　Heroes of what they dream, but never tell;
Father, in your vast playground let them know
　The loveliness of ocean, star and hill;
Protect from every bitterness and woe
　Your heedless little acolytes, and still
Grant me the grace, I beg upon my knees,
Not to forget that I was one of these.

—Arthur Guiterman.

205

PRAYER OF AN OUTDOOR MAN

With the leafy branches of the forest trees I lift my arms to pray; with the babbling brooks and singing birds I raise my voice in praise:

I thank Thee for the out-of-doors;

I thank Thee for the solitude of wild places, the strength of the hills and the calmness of quiet streams;

I thank Thee for old clothes, rough work, and the right to let my beard grow;

I thank Thee for the curling smoke of a campfire in the early morning;

I thank Thee for steaming coffee, sizzling bacon and an outdoor appetite;

I thank Thee for the swish of my paddle, and the joy of watching fleecy clouds roll by;

I thank Thee for the call of a whippoorwill at dusk, across a silent lake;

I thank Thee for silvery moonbeams on rippling water;

I thank Thee for the singing of my reel and the bending of my rod as a Big One strikes;

I thank Thee for the contentment that comes with the patter of rain on my tent at night;

I thank Thee for wild blackberries along an old stump fence;

I thank Thee for my dogs, my gun, and the flaming colors of the autumn woods;

I thank Thee for wild ducks flying south against a dull grey sky;

I thank Thee for the glory and majesty of the stars;

I thank Thee for strong winds pulling at my hair roots and for the spray from the lake on my cheeks;

I thank Thee for old trails, for rocks, for raging rapids and for a glimpse of deer drinking in a secluded pool;

I thank Thee for the drum of the partridge, for squirrels, trailing arbutus, the aroma of pine needles, sunshine through the leaves, and all the other eternal miracles of the out-of-doors.

—*Wilferd Peterson.*

206

PRAYER

I kneel not now to pray that Thou
    Make white one single sin—
I only kneel to thank the Lord
    For what I have not been;

For deeds which sprouted in my heart
    But ne'er to bloom were brought,
For monstrous vices which I slew
    In the shambles of my thought—

Dark deeds the world has never guessed
    By hell and passion bred,
Which never grew beyond the bud
    That cankered in my head.

Some said I was a righteous man—
    Poor fools! The gallows tree
(If Thou hadst let one foot to slip)
    Had held a limb for me.

So for the man I might have been
    My heart must cease to mourn,
'Twere best to praise the living God
    For monsters never born;

To bend the spiritual knee
(Knowing myself within)
And thank the kind, benignant God
For what I have not been!

—*Harry Kemp.*

207

A BOY SPEAKS

Dear God: *He* was an old-man dog. . . .
Here is his bowl and his pillow.
We buried him this morning
Beneath the garden willow. . . .

If terriers go to Heaven—
It's raining so tonight,
Please whistle, God, and pet him
Until he seems all right. . . .

God, if he will not eat,
But maybe just stands still—
Please pick him up a little
And talk to him until

He wags his tail against you,
Then let him lick your chin.
He was *my* dog . . . (Old Buddy)
Please, God . . . please take him in.

—*Queene B. Lister.*

208

THE AWAKENING

I could not pray as one should pray
   Nor trust as one should trust,
Until sin took my boasted strength
   And dragged it in the dust.

I could not pity those who fall,
   Until as they I fell—
God has so many different ways
   To save a soul from hell!
              —Whitney Montgomery.

209

BANKRUPT

One midnight, deep in starlight still,
I dreamed that I received this bill:
(——— in account with Life):
Five thousand breathless dawns all new;
Five thousand sunsets wrapped in gold;
One million snow-flakes served ice-cold;
Five quiet friends; one baby's love;
One white-mad sea with clouds above;
One hundred music-haunted dreams
Of moon-drenched roads and hurrying streams;
Of prophesying winds, and trees;
Of silent stars and browsing bees;
One June night in a fragrant wood;
One heart that loved and understood.
I wondered when I waked at day,
How—how in God's name—I could pay!
              —Cortlandt W. Sayres.

210

THE FEAR OF DEATH

Last night I woke and found between us drawn—
  Between us, where no mortal fear may creep—
  The vision of Death dividing us in sleep;
And suddenly I thought, Ere light shall dawn
Some day,—the substance, not the shadow, of Death
  Shall cleave us like a sword. The vision passed,
  But all its new-born horror held me fast,
And till day broke I listened for your breath.
Some day to wake, and find that coloured skies,
  And pipings in the woods, and petals wet,
  Are things for aching memory to forget;
And that your living hands and mouth and eyes
Are part of all the world's old histories!—
  Dear God! a little longer, ah, not yet!

                —*Edmund Gosse.*

211

NO PILOTS WE

Would I were one of those who preach no Cause—
Nor guide mankind with meddling fingertips;
But let each star that moves without a pause
Shine as it list—as potent when it dips
Beyond their ken in visual eclipse
As when it blazes in a darkling sky,
Regnant and beautiful, while with mute lips
Men bow the head in worship, or in shy
And inexpressive words admit that God is nigh.

We are no pilots: let us trust our bark,
Miraculous, alert, not made with hands,
That feels a magic impulse through the dark,
And leaps upon the course it understands
From shores unknown to unimagined strands;
Resists the helm we give it, but divines—
Being itself divine—divine commands;
And answers to no compass save the signs
Encircling deepest heaven where the Zodiac shines.
—*John Jay Chapman.*

212

A SINNER CONTEMPLATES

When all this life is suddenly quite done,
If I should meet with God, some April day,
Will He recall I hadn't time to pray
Or go to church, and sigh, "So, you're the one."

Or will He overlook that little thing,
And pause beside me, neighborlike and say,
"The daffodils are doing well this spring."
—*Frances Boal Mehlek.*

213

INSCRIPTIONS AT THE CITY OF BRASS

From the *Thousand and One Nights*
Translated from the Arabic by *Edward Powys Mathers*

.   .   .

I had ten thousand horses
Groomed by captive kings,
I had a thousand virgins of royal blood

To serve my pleasure
And a thousand excellent virgins
With moon-colored breasts,
Chosen from all the world.
They brought forth little princes in my chambers
And the little princes were as brave as lions.
I had peculiar treasures
And the West and the East were two heads
Bowing before me.
I thought my power eternal
And the days of my life
Fixed surely in the years;
But a whisper came to me
From Him who dies not.
I called my captains and my strong riders,
Thousands upon thousands
With swords and lances;
I called my tributary kings together
And those who were proud rulers under me,
I opened the boxes of my treasure to them, saying:
"Take hills of gold, mountains of silver,
And give me one more day upon the earth."
But they stood silent,
Looking upon the ground;
So that I died
And death came to sit upon my throne.
I was Kush bin Shadad bin Ad,
Surnamed the Great.

.   .   .

XV

THE STAG AND HIS DREAMS

I never envy millionaires
    With their wealth and motor cars—
I'd like to be a poet, though,
    For they own all the stars.

214

THE CRY OF THE DREAMER

I am tired of planning and toiling
  In the crowded hives of men,
Heart-weary of building and spoiling,
  And spoiling and building again,
And I long for the dear old river,
  Where I dreamed my youth away;
For a dreamer lives forever,
  And a toiler dies in a day.

I am sick of the showy seeming,
  Of life that is half a lie;
Of the faces lined with scheming
  In the throng that hurries by;
From the sleepless thought's endeavor
  I would go where the children play;
For a dreamer lives forever,
  And a thinker dies in a day.

I can feel no pride, but pity,
  For the burdens the rich endure;
There is nothing sweet in the city
  But the patient lives of the poor.
Oh, the little hands too skillful,
  And the child-mind choked with weeds!
The daughter's heart grown willful
  And the father's heart that bleeds!

No! no! from the streets' rude bustle,
  From trophies of mart and stage,
I would fly to the wood's low rustle
  And the meadows' kindly page.

Let me dream as of old by the river,
  And be loved for my dreams alway;
For a dreamer lives forever,
  And a toiler dies in a day.
                —*John Boyle O'Reilly.*

215

TO A POET A THOUSAND YEARS HENCE

I who am dead a thousand years,
  And wrote this sweet archaic song,
Send you my words for messengers
  The way I shall not pass along.

I care not if you bridge the seas,
  Or ride secure the cruel sky,
Or build consummate palaces
  Of metal or of masonry.

But have you wine and music still,
  And statues and a bright-eyed love,
And foolish thoughts of good and ill,
  And prayers to them who sit above?

How shall we conquer? Like a wind
  That falls at eve our fancies blow,
And old Maeonides the blind
  Said it three thousand years ago.

O friend unseen, unborn, unknown,
  Student of our sweet English tongue,
Read out my words at night, alone:
  I was a poet, I was young.

Since I can never see your face,
 And never shake you by the hand,
I send my soul through time and space
 To greet you. You will understand.
 —*James Elroy Flecker.*

216

A PHANTASY OF HEAVEN

Perhaps he plays with cherubs now,
 Those little, golden boys of God,
Bending with them, some silver bough,
 The while a seraph, head a-nod,

Slumbers on guard; how they will run
 And shout, if he should wake too soon,—
As fruit more golden than the sun
 And riper than the full-grown moon,

Conglobed in clusters, weighs them down,
 Like Atlas heaped with starry signs;
And, if they're tripped, heel over crown,
 By hidden coils of mighty vines,—

Perhaps the seraph, swift to pounce,
 Will hale them, vexed, to God—and He
Will only laugh, remembering, once
 He was a boy in Galilee!
 —*Harry Kemp.*

217

SOMETIMES

Across the fields of yesterday
　　He sometimes comes to me,
A little lad just back from play—
　　The lad I used to be.

And yet he smiles so wistfully
　　Once he has crept within,
I wonder if he hopes to see
　　The man I might have been.
　　　　　　　—*Thomas S. Jones, Jr.*

218

YOU HELPED THE DUMB

Just in a dream I stood at Heaven's gate,
St. Peter met me with his Book of Fate—
A pond'rous volume bound in glist'ning gold,
With letters large that stood out clear and bold;
He thought awhile, then shook his hoary head—
"The records show but few good deeds," he said.
"And not enough to merit Heaven, I fear;
To me your prospects, friend, look rather drear."
He traced the scanty items with his thumb,
When, lo! he stopped and said, "You helped the dumb—
You took a stray cat in, two dogs you fed,
And to the birds you gave some crusts of bread.

Ah, yes! you did your best to aid the weak,
God's little folk, the ones that could not speak;
So enter, thou, and join the angel-band,
There is a place for you at God's right hand."

—*Willa Hoey.*

219

ABOU BEN ADHEM

Abou Ben Adhem (may his tribe increase!)
Awoke one night from a deep dream of peace,
And saw within the moonlight in his room,
Making it rich and like a lily in bloom,
An angel writing in a book of gold:
Exceeding peace had made Ben Adhem bold,
And to the presence in the room he said,
"What writest thou?" The vision raised its head,
And, with a look made of all sweet accord,
Answered, "The names of those who love the Lord."
"And is mine one?" said Abou. "Nay, not so,"
Replied the angel. Abou spoke more low,
But cheerily still; and said, "I pray thee, then,
Write me as one that loves his fellow-men."

The angel wrote, and vanished. The next night
It came again, with a great wakening light,
And showed the names whom love of god had blessed,—
And, lo! Ben Adhem's name led all the rest!

—*James Henry Leigh Hunt.*

220

KINSHIP

I am part of the sea and stars
    And the winds of the South and North,
Of mountain and moon and mars,
    And the ages sent me forth!

Blind Homer, the splendor of Greece,
    Sang the songs I sang here he fell;
She whom men called Beatrice,
    Saw me in the depths of hell.

I was hanged at dawn for a crime—
    Flesh dies, but the soul knows no death;
I piped to great Shakespeare's chime
    The witches' song in Macbeth.

All, all who have suffered and won,
    Who have struggled and failed and died,
Am I, with work still undone,
    And a spear-mark in my side.

I am part of the sea and stars
    And the winds of the South and North
Of mountains and moon and Mars,
    And the ages sent me forth!

                            —*Edward H. S. Terry.*

221

THE FOOL'S PRAYER

The royal feast was done; the King
  Sought some new sport to banish care,
And to his jester cried: "Sir Fool,
  Kneel now, and make for us a prayer!"

The jester doffed his cap and bells,
  And stood the mocking court before;
They could not see the bitter smile
  Behind the painted grin he wore.

He bowed his head, and bent his knee
  Upon the monarch's silken stool;
His pleading voice arose: "O Lord,
  Be merciful to me, a fool!

"No pity, Lord, could change the heart
  From red with wrong to white as wool;
The rod must heal the sin: but, Lord,
  Be merciful to me, a fool!

" 'Tis not by guilt the onward sweep
  Of truth and right, O Lord, we stay;
'Tis by our follies that so long
  We hold the earth from heaven away.

"These clumsy feet, still in the mire,
  Go crushing blossoms without end;
These hard, well-meaning hands we thrust
  Among the heart-strings of a friend.

"The ill-timed truth we might have kept—
  Who knows how sharp it pierced and stung?
The word we had not sense to say—
  Who knows how grandly it had rung?

"Our faults no tenderness should ask,
  The chastening stripes must cleanse them all;
But for our blunders—oh, in shame
  Before the eyes of heaven we fall.

"Earth bears no balsam for mistakes;
  Men crown the knave, and scourge the tool
That did his will; but Thou, O Lord,
  Be merciful to me, a fool!"

The room was hushed; in silence rose
  The King, and sought his gardens cool,
And walked apart, and murmured low,
  "Be merciful to me, a fool!"
                    —*Edward Rowland Sill.*

222

MEMORY

My mind lets go a thousand things,
Like dates of wars and deaths of kings,
And yet recalls the very hour—
'Twas noon by yonder village tower,
And on the last blue noon in May—
The wind came briskly up this way,

Crisping the brook beside the road;
Then, pausing here, set down its load
Of pine-scents, and shook listlessly
Two petals from that wild-rose tree.
  —*Thomas Bailey Aldrich.*

223

THE GHOSTS OF THE BUFFALOES

Last night at black midnight I woke with a cry.
The windows were shaking, there was thunder on high,
The floor was a-tremble, the door was a-jar,
White fires, crimson fires, shone from afar.
I rushed to the dooryard. The city was gone.
My home was a hut without orchard or lawn.
It was mud-smear and logs near a whispering stream,
Nothing else built by man could I see in my dream . . .

Then . . .
Ghost-kings came headlong, row upon row,
Gods of the Indians, torches aglow.
They mounted the bear and the elk and the deer,
And eagles gigantic, agèd and sere,
They rode long-horn cattle, they cried "A-la-la."
They lifted the knife, the bow and the spear,
They lifted ghost-torches from dead fires below,
The midnight made grand with the cry "A-la-la."
The midnight made grand with a red-god charge,
A red-god show,
A red-god show,
"A-la-la, a-la-la, a-la-la, a-la-la."

With bodies like bronze, and terrible eyes
Came the rank and the file, with catamount cries,
Gibbering, yipping, with hollow-skull clacks,
Riding white bronchos with skeleton backs,
Scalp-hunters, beaded and spangled and bad,
Naked and lustful and foaming and mad,
Flashing primeval demoniac scorn,
Blood-thirst and pomp amid darkness reborn,
Power and glory that sleep in the grass
While the winds and the snows and the great rains pass.
They crossed the gray river, thousands abreast,
They rode out in infinite lines to the west,
Tide upon tide of strange fury and foam,
Spirits and wraiths, the blue was their home,
The sky was their goal where the star-flags are furled,
And on past those far golden splendors they whirled.
They burned to dim meteors, lost in the deep,
And I turned in dazed wonder, thinking of sleep.

And the wind crept by
Alone, unkempt, unsatisfied,
The wind cried and cried—
Muttered of massacres long past,
Buffaloes in shambles vast . . .
An owl said, "Hark, what is a-wing?"
I heard a cricket caroling,
I heard a cricket caroling,
I heard a cricket caroling.

Then . . .
Snuffing the lightning that crashed from on high
Rose royal old buffaloes, row upon row.
The lords of the prairie came galloping by.
And I cried in my heart "A-la-la, a-la-la.

A red-god show,
A red-god show,
A-la-la, a-la-la, a-la-la."

Buffaloes, buffaloes, thousands abreast,
A scourge and amazement, they swept to the west.
With black bobbing noses, with red rolling tongues,
Coughing forth steam from their leather-wrapped lungs,
Cows with their calves, bulls big and vain,
Goring the laggards, shaking the mane,
Stamping flint feet, flashing moon eyes,
Pompous and owlish, shaggy and wise.

Like sea-cliffs and caves resounded their ranks
With shoulders lives waves, and undulant flanks.
Tide upon tide of strange fury and foam,
Spirits and wraiths, the blue was their home,
The sky was their goal where the star-flags are furled,
And on past those far golden splendors they whirled.
They burned to dim meteors, lost in the deep,
And I turned in dazed wonder, thinking of sleep.

I heard a cricket's cymbals play,
A scarecrow lightly flapped his rags,
And a pan that hung by his shoulder rang,
Rattled and thumped in a listless way,
And now the wind in the chimney sang,
The wind in the chimney,
The wind in the chimney,
The wind in the chimney,
Seemed to say:—
"Dream, boy, dream,

If you anywise can.
To dream is the work
Of beast or man.

Life is the west-going dream-storm's breath,
Life is a dream, the sigh of the skies,
The breath of the stars, that nod on their pillows
With their golden hair mussed over their eyes."
The locust played on his musical wing,
Sang to his mate of love's delight.
I heard the whippoorwill's soft fret.
I heard a cricket caroling,
I heard a cricket caroling,
I heard a cricket say: "Good-night, good-night,
Good-night, good-night, . . . good-night."

—Vachel Lindsay.

224

I HEAR AMERICA SINGING

I hear America singing, the varied carols I hear,
Those of mechanics, each one singing his as it should be
    blithe and strong,
The carpenter singing his as he measures his plank or beam,
The mason singing his as he makes ready for work, or leaves
    off work,
The boatman singing what belongs to him in his boat, the
    deck-hand singing on the steamboat deck,
The shoemaker singing as he sits on his bench, the hatter
    singing as he stands,
The wood-cutters' song, the ploughboy's on his way in the
    morning, or at noon intermission or at sundown,

The delicious singing of the mother, or of the young wife at
    work, or of the girl sewing or washing,
Each singing what belongs to him or her and to none else,
The day what belongs to the day—at night the party of
    young fellows, robust, friendly,
Singing with open mouths their strong melodious songs.

                     —*Walt Whitman.*

XVI

HOME FROM THE HILL

This be the verse you grave for me:
Here he lies where he longed to be;
Home is the sailor, home from sea,
   And the hunter home from the hill.

              —*Robert Louis Stevenson.*

225

THE OLD SONG

When all the world is young, lad,
   And all the trees are green;
And every goose a swan, lad,
   And every lass a queen;
Then hey for boot and horse, lad,
   And round the world away!
Young blood must have its course, lad,
   And every dog his day.

When all the world is old, lad,
   And all the trees are brown;
And all the sport is stale, lad,
   And all the wheels run down;
Creep home, and take your place there
   The spent and maim'd among;
God grant you find one face there
   You loved when all was young!
                —Charles Kingsley.

226

SOLITUDE

Happy the man, whose wish and care
A few paternal acres bound,
Content to breathe his native air
              In his own ground.

Whose herds with milk, whose fields with bread
Whose flocks supply him with attire;
Whose trees in summer yield him shade,
              In winter fire.

Blest, who can unconcern'dly find
Hours, days, and years, slide soft away
In health of body, peace of mind,
                    Quiet by day.

Sound sleep by night; study and ease
Together mix'd, sweet recreation,
And innocence, which most does please
                    With meditation.

Thus let me live, unseen, unknown;
Thus unlamented let me die;
Steal from the world, and not a stone
                    Tell where I lie.
                    —*Alexander Pope.*

227

THE STAY-AT-HOME

You may sing your songs to the frozen North,
  To the land of the hidden gold,
Where the snow-capped mountains mutely bid
  A challenge to those who are bold.

You may sing your songs to the torrid South,
  Where fevers will madden the brain,
Where only the men of the staunchest stuff
  Are fit to return home again.

You may sing your songs to the desert waste,
  To treks o'er the blistering sands;
You may sing your songs to hunger and thirst
  In the depths of far-away lands.

But don't forget when you're speaking about
   The countries where virile men roam
To mention, in passing, a word of praise
   To the brave souls who stay at home.

There's courage required of those who defy
   The dangers and hardships unseen,
But there's courage, too, in the heart of those
   Who stick to the daily routine.

For it takes a heart that is stout and strong
   To stand the monotonous ways
Of a Life that is fraught with drab events
   In a City of Changeless Days.
           —*Robert W. Kernaghan.*

228

TO-MORROW

In the downhill of life, when I find I'm declining,
   May my fate no less fortunate be
Than a snug elbow-chair can afford for reclining,
   And a cot that o'er looks the wide sea;
With an ambling pad-pony to pace o'er the lawn,
   While I carol away idle sorrow,
And blithe as the lark that each day hails the dawn
   Look forward with hope for to-morrow.

With a porch at my door, both for shelter and shade too,
   As the sun-shine or rain may prevail;
And a small spot of ground for the use of the spade too,
   With a barn for the use of the flail:

A cow for my dairy, a dog for my game,
  And a purse when a friend wants to borrow;
I'll envy no nabob his riches or fame,
  Nor what honors may wait him to-morrow.

From the bleak northern blast may my cot be completely
  Secured by a neighboring hill;
And at night may repose steal upon me more sweetly
  By the sound of a murmuring rill:
And while peace and plenty I find at my board,
  With a heart free from sickness and sorrow,
With my friends may I share what to-day may afford,
  And let them spread the table to-morrow.

And when I at last must throw off this frail covering
  Which I've worn for three-score years and ten,
On the brink of the grave I'll not seek to keep hovering,
  Nor my thread wish to spin o'er again:
But my face in the glass I'll serenely survey,
  And with smiles count each wrinkle and furrow;
And this old worn-out stuff, which is threadbare to-day,
  May become everlasting to-morrow.

                              —*J. Collins.*

229

THE LAY OF THE LAST MINSTREL

.   .   .

Breathes there the man, with soul so dead,
Who never to himself hath said,
  This is my own, my native land!
Whose heart hath ne'er within him burned,
As home his footsteps he hath turned,

From wandering on a foreign strand!
If such there breathe, go, mark him well;
For him no Minstrel raptures swell;
High though his titles, proud his name,
Boundless his wealth as wish can claim;
Despite those titles, power, and pelf,
The wretch, concentred all in self,
Living, shall forfeit fair renown,
And, doubly dying, shall go down
To the vile dust, from whence he sprung,
Unwept, unhonoured, and unsung.

.   .   .

—*Sir Walter Scott.*

230

AMERICA FOR ME

'Tis fine to see the Old World and travel up and down
Among the famous palaces and cities of renown,
To admire the crumbly castles and the statues of the kings
But now I think I've had enough of antiquated things.

So it's home again, and home again, America for me!
My heart is turning home again and there I long to be,
In the land of youth and freedom, beyond the ocean bars,
Where the air is full of sunlight and the flag is full of stars.

Oh, London is a man's town, there's power in the air;
And Paris is a woman's town, with flowers in her hair;
And it's sweet to dream in Venice, and it's great to study
    Rome;
But when it comes to living there is no place like home.

I like the German fir-woods in green battalions drilled;
I like the gardens of Versailles with flashing fountains
    filled;
But, oh, to take your hand, my dear, and ramble for a day
In the friendly western woodland where Nature has her
    sway!

I know that Europe's wonderful, yet something seems to
    lack!
The Past is too much with her, and the people looking back.
But the glory of the Present is to make the Future free—
We love our land for what she is and what she is to be.

Oh, it's home again, and home again, America for me!
I want a ship that's westward bound to plough the rolling
    sea,
To the blessed Land of Room Enough, beyond the ocean
    bars,
Where the air is full of sunlight and the flag is full of stars.

                          —*Henry Van Dyke.*

XVII

ALL PASSION SPENT

I know the night is near at hand.
  The mists lie low on hill and bay,
The autumn sheaves are dewless, dry;
  But I have had the day.

—S. *Weir Mitchell.*

231

FINIS

When the dust of the workshop is still,
The dust of the workman at rest,
May some generous heart find a will
To seek and to treasure his best.

From the splendour of hopes that deceived;
From the wonders he planned to do;
From the glories so nearly achieved;
From the dreams that so nearly came true.

From his struggle to rise above earth
On the pinions that could not fly;
From his sorrows, oh, seek for some worth
To remember the workman by.

If in vain; if Time sweeps all away,
And no laurel from that dust springs;
'Tis enough that a loyal heart say,
"He tried to make beautiful things."
                              —*Eden Phillpotts.*

232

YOUTH AND AGE

Verse, a breeze 'mid blossoms straying,
Where Hope clung feeding, like a bee—
Both were mine! Life went a-maying
  With Nature, Hope, and Poesy,
    When I was young!

When I was young?—Ah, woeful when!
Ah! for the change 'twixt Now and Then!
This breathing house not built with hands,
This body that does me grievous wrong,
O'er aery cliffs and glittering sands
How lightly then it flash'd along:
Like those trim skiffs, unknown of yore,
On winding lakes and rivers wide,
That ask no aid of sail or oar,
That fear no spite of wind or tide!
Nought cared this body for wind or weather
When Youth and I lived in't together.

. . .

—*S. T. Coleridge.*

233

ON THE TOMBS IN WESTMINSTER ABBEY

. . .

Mortality, behold, and fear,
What a change of flesh is here!
Think how many royal bones
Sleep within this heap of stones;
Here they lie, had realms and lands,
Who now want strength to stir their hands;
Where from their pulpits seal'd with dust,
They preach, "In greatness is no trust!"
Here's an acre sown indeed
With the richest, royal'st seed,
That the earth did e'er suck in
Since the first man died for sin;

Here the bones of birth have cried,
"Though gods they were, as men they died";
Here are sands, ignoble things
Dropt from the ruin'd sides of kings.
Here's a world of pomp and state
Buried in dust, once dead by fate!

—Francis Beaumont.

234

"FAME IS A FOOD THAT DEAD MEN EAT"

Fame is a food that dead men eat,—
I have no stomach for such meat.
In little light and narrow room,
They eat it in the silent tomb,
With no kind voice of comrade near
To bid the banquet be of cheer.

But Friendship is a nobler thing,—
Of Friendship it is good to sing.
For truly, when a man shall end,
He lives in memory of his friend,
Who doth his better part recall,
And of his faults make funeral.

—Austin Dobson.

235

THE OLD FAMILIAR FACES

I have had playmates, I have had companions
In my days of childhood, in my joyful school-days;
All, all are gone, the old familiar faces.

I have been laughing, I have been carousing,
Drinking late, sitting late, with my bosom cronies;
All, all are gone, the old familiar faces.

I loved a Love once, fairest among women:
Closed are her doors on me, I must not see her—
All, all are gone, the old familiar faces.

I have a friend, a kinder friend has no man:
Like an ingrate, I left my friend abruptly;
Left him, to muse on the old familiar faces.

Ghost-like I paced round the haunts of my childhood,
Earth seem'd a desert I was bound to traverse,
Seeking to find the old familiar faces.

Friend of my bosom, thou more than a brother,
Why wert not thou born in my father's dwelling?
So might we talk of the old familiar faces,

How some they have died, and some they have left
    me,
And some are taken from me; all are departed;
All, all are gone, the old familiar faces.

—Charles Lamb

236
THE LIGHT OF OTHER DAYS

.   .   .

When I remember all
    The friends so link'd together
I've seen around me fall
    Like leaves in wintry weather,

I feel like one
Who treads alone
Some banquet-hall deserted,
Whose lights are fled
Whose garlands dead,
And all but he departed!
Thus in the stilly night
Ere slumber's chain has bound me,
Sad Memory brings the light
Of other days around me.

—*Thomas Moore.*

237

PAST AND PRESENT

.   .   .

I remember, I remember
The fir-trees dark and high;
I used to think their slender tops
Were close against the sky:
It was a childish ignorance,
But now 'tis little joy
To know I'm farther off from Heaven
Than when I was a boy.

—*Thomas Hood.*

238

THE MURDERED TRAVELLER

When Spring, to woods and wastes around,
Brought bloom and joy again,
The murdered traveller's bones were found,
Far down a narrow glen.

The fragrant birch, above him, hung
Her tassels in the sky;
And many a vernal blossom sprung,
And nodded careless by.

The red-bird warbled as he wrought
His hanging nest o'erhead,
And fearless, near the fatal spot,
Her young the partridge led.

But there was weeping far away,
And gentle eyes, for him,
With watching many an anxious day,
Were sorrowful and dim.

They little knew, who loved him so,
The fearful death he met,
When shouting o'er the desert snow,
Unarmed, and hard beset;—

Nor how, when round the frosty pole
The northern dawn was red,
The mountain-wolf and wild-cat stole
To banquet on the dead;—

Nor how, when strangers found his bones,
They dressed the hasty bier,
And marked his grave with nameless tones,
Unmoistened by a tear.

But long they looked, and feared, and wept,
Within his distant home;
And dreamed, and started as they slept,
For joy that he was come.

Long, long they looked—but never spied
His welcome step again,
Nor knew the fearful death he died
Far down that narrow glen.
                    —*William Cullen Bryant.*

239
HAMLET

To be, or not to be: that is the question:
Whether 'tis nobler in the mind to suffer
The slings and arrows of outrageous fortune,
Or to take arms against a sea of troubles,
And by opposing end them? To die: to sleep;
No more; and, by a sleep to say we end
The heart-ache and the thousand natural shocks
That flesh is heir to, 'tis a consummation
Devoutly to be wish'd. To die, to sleep;
To sleep: perchance to dream: ay, there's the rub;
For in that sleep of death what dreams may come
When we have shuffled off this mortal coil,
Must give us pause. There's the respect
That makes calamity of so long life;
For who would bear the whips and scorns of time,
The oppressor's wrong, the proud man's contumely,
The pangs of dispriz'd love, the law's delay,
The insolence of office, and the spurns
That patient merit of the unworthy takes,
When he himself might his quietus make
With a bare bodkin? who would fardels bear,
To grunt and sweat under a weary life,
But that the dread of something after death,
The undiscover'd country from whose bourn

No traveller returns, puzzles the will,
And makes us rather bear those ills we have
Than fly to others that we know not of?
Thus conscience does make cowards of us all;
And thus the native hue of resolution
Is sicklied o'er with the pale cast of thought,
And enterprises of great pith and moment
With this regard their currents turn awry,
And lose the name of action.

·   ·   ·

—*Shakespeare.*

240

KING HENRY THE EIGHTH

Farewell! a long farewell, to all my greatness!
This is the state of man: to-day he puts forth
The tender leaves of hopes; to-morrow blossoms,
And bears his blushing honours thick upon him;
The third day comes a frost, a killing frost;
And, when he thinks, good easy man, full surely
His greatness is a-ripening, nips his root,
And then he falls, as I do. I have ventur'd,
Like little wanton boys that swim on bladders,
This many summers in a sea of glory,
But far beyond my depth: my high-blown pride
At length broke under me, and now has left me,
Weary and old with service, to the mercy
Of a rude stream, that must for ever hide me.

·   ·   ·

—*Shakespeare.*

241

RICHARD THE SECOND

   . . . Of comfort no man speak:
Let's talk of graves, of worms, and epitaphs;
Make dust our paper, and with rainy eyes
Write sorrow on the bosom of the earth;
Let's choose executors and talk of wills:
And yet no so—for what can we bequeath
Save our deposed bodies to the ground?
Our lands, our lives, and all are Bolingbroke's,
And nothing can we call our own but death,
And that small model of the barren earth
Which serves as paste and cover to our bones.
For God's sake, let us sit upon the ground
And tell sad stories of the death of kings:
How some have been depos'd, some slain in war,
Some haunted by the ghosts they have depos'd,
Some poison'd by their wives, some sleeping kill'd;
All murder'd: for within the hollow crown
That rounds the mortal temples of a king
Keeps Death his court, and there the antick sits,
Scoffing his state and grinning at his pomp;
Allowing him a breath, a little scene,
To monarchize, be fear'd, and kill with looks,
Infusing him with self and vain conceit
As if this flesh which walls about our life
Were brass impregnable; and humour'd thus
Comes at the last, and with a little pin
Bores through his castle wall, and farewell king!
Cover your heads, and mock not flesh and blood
With solemn reverence: throw away respect,
Tradition, form, and ceremonious duty,
For you have but mistook me all this while:

I live with bread like you, feel want,
Taste grief, need friends: subjected thus,
How can you say to me I am a king?

—*Shakespeare.*

242

MACBETH

. . .

To-morrow, and to-morrow, and to-morrow,
Creeps in this petty pace from day to day,
To the last syllable of recorded time;
And all our yesterdays have lighted fools
The way to dusty death. Out, out, brief candle!
Life's but a walking shadow, a poor player
That struts and frets his hour upon the stage,
And then is heard no more; it is a tale
Told by an idiot, full of sound and fury,
Signifying nothing.

—*Shakespeare.*

243

OUR REVELS NOW ARE ENDED

Our revels now are ended. These our actors,
As I foretold you, were all spirits and
Are melted into air, into thin air:
And, like the baseless fabric of this vision,
The cloud-capp'd towers, the gorgeous palaces,
The solemn temples, the great globe itself,
Yea, all which it inherit, shall dissolve

And, like this insubstantial pageant faded,
Leave not a rack behind. We are such stuff
As dreams are made on, and our little life
Is rounded with a sleep.

>—*Shakespeare.*

244

THE GARDEN OF PROSERPINE

. . . From too much love of living,
    From hope and fear set free,
We thank with brief thanksgiving
    Whatever gods may be,
That no life lives forever;
That dead men rise up never;
That even the weariest river
    Winds somewhere safe to sea . . .

>—*Algernon Swinburne.*

245

MY TRIUMPH

Let the thick curtain fall;
I better know than all
How little I have gained,
How vast the unattained.

Not by the page word-painted
Let life be banned or sainted:
Deeper than written scroll
The colors of the soul.

Sweeter than any sung
My songs have found no tongue
Nobler than any fact
My wish that failed to act.

Others shall sing the song,
Others shall right the wrong,—
Finish what I begin
And all I fail of win.

What matter, I or they?
Mine or another's day,
So the right word be said
And life the sweeter made

Hail to the coming singers!
Hail to the brave light-bringers!
Forward I reach and share
All that they sing and dare.

The airs of heaven blow o'er me;
A glory shines before me
Of what mankind shall be,—
Pure, generous, brave, and free.

A dream of man and woman
Diviner but still human,
Solving the riddle old,
Shaping the Age of Gold!

The love of God and neighbor;
An equal-handed labor;
The richer life, where beauty
Walks hand in hand with duty.

Ring, bells in unreared steeples,
The joy of unborn peoples!
Sound, trumpets far off blown,
Your triumph is my own.

Parcel and part of all,
I keep the festival,
Fore-reach the good to be,
And share the victory.

I feel the earth move sunward,
I join the great march onward,
And take, by faith, while living,
My freehold of thanksgiving.
    —John Greenleaf Whittier.

246
TIMES GO BY TURNS

The loppèd tree in time may grow again,
Most naked plants renew both fruit and flower;
The sorest wight may find release of pain,
The driest soil suck in some moist'ning shower:
Times go by turns and chances change by course,
From foul to fair, from better hap to worse.

The sea of Fortune doth not ever flow,
She draws her favours to the lowest ebb;
Her time hath equal times to come and go,
Her loom doth weave the fine and coarsest web;
No joy so great but runneth to an end,
No hap so hard but may in fine amend.

Not always fall of leaf nor ever spring,
No endless night yet not eternal day;
The saddest birds a season find to sing,
The roughest storm a calm may soon allay:
Thus with succeeding turns God tempereth all,
That man may hope to rise, yet fear to fall.

A chance may win that by mischance was lost;
The net that holds no great, takes little fish;
In some things all, in all things none are crost,
Few all they need, but none have all they wish;
Unmeddled joys here to no man befall:
Who least, hath some; who most, hath never all.

—*Robert Southwell.*

247

THE DAY IS DONE

The day is done, and the darkness
  Falls from the wings of Night,
As a feather is wafted downward
  From an eagle in his flight.

I see the lights of the village
  Gleam through the rain and the mist,
And a feeling of sadness comes o'er me
  That my soul cannot resist:

A feeling of sadness and longing,
  That is not akin to pain,

And resembles sorrow only
  As the mist resembles rain.

Come, read to me some poem,
  Some simple and heartfelt lay,
That shall soothe this restless feeling,
  And banish the thoughts of day.

Not from the grand old masters,
  Not from the bards sublime,
Whose distant footsteps echo
  Through the corridors of Time.

For, like strains of martial music,
  Their mighty thoughts suggest
Life's endless toil and endeavor;
  And tonight I long for rest.

Read from some humbler poet,
  Whose songs gushed from his heart,
As showers from the clouds of summer,
  Or tears from the eyelids start;

Who, through long days of labor,
  And nights devoid of ease,
Still heard in his soul the music
  Of wonderful melodies.

Such songs have power to quiet
  The restless pulse of care,
And come like the benediction
  That follows after prayer.

Then read from the treasured volume
    The poem of thy choice,
And lend to the rhyme of the poet
    The beauty of thy voice.

.   .   .

—*Henry Wadsworth Longfellow.*

248

GOOD-BYE

Good-bye, proud world! I'm going home:
Thou art not my friend, and I'm not thine.
Long through thy weary crowds I roam;
A river-ark on the ocean brine,
Long I've been tossed like the driven foam;
But now, proud world! I'm going home.

Good-bye to Flattery's fawning face;
To Grandeur with his wise grimace;
To upstart Wealth's averted eye;
To supple Office, low and high;
To crowded halls, to court and street;
To frozen hearts and hasting feet;
To those who go, and those who come;
Good-bye, proud world! I'm going home.

I am going to my own hearth-stone,
Bosomed in yon green hills alone,—
A secret nook in a pleasant land,
Whose groves the frolic fairies planned;
Where arches green, the livelong day,
Echo the blackbird's roundelay,

And vulgar feet have never trod
A spot that is sacred to thought and God.

O, when I am safe in my sylvan home,
I tread on the pride of Greece and Rome;
And when I am stretched beneath the pines,
Where the evening star so holy shines,
I laugh at the lore and the pride of man,
At the sophist schools and the learned clan;
For what are they all, in their high conceit,
When a man in the bush with God may meet?
                        —*Ralph Waldo Emerson.*

249

BEACHCOMBER

My life like sand at the ebb tide seems
    With nothing but driftwood in reach;
The shattered bits of a thousand dreams,
    And I am a comber along the beach.

But once I sailed from the furthest seas
    And fathomed the deepest streams
On a ship I conned in the gale and breeze
    And christened it ship of dreams.

My ship of dreams was a sturdy ship
    When it first ventured out to sea
With dreams enough for a life-long trip
    To the port of eternity.

But the ports are many that lie between,
  And I've lingered in every one
Where my dreams grew small and my heart less
  keen
  For the sea where my dreams were spun.

And I left a dream in each port of call,
  Deep buried without a shroud,
Now I haven't one single dream at all
  Of the cargo that once was proud.

My ship of dreams is a haunted ship
  That I sail when the moon rides low,
For my dreams have suffered complete collapse,
  But I don't want the moon to know.

               —*Harcourt Strange.*

250

FARM FUNERAL

The man who breaks and tills the sod
Works in full partnership with God;
One single thought, plan matching plan,
The unity of God and man—
No finer tribute can be paid
To any dead than this; he made
A barren field to bloom, his hand
Brought fruitfulness unto the land.

The strong brown hands are quiet now,
That knew the secrets of the plow—
In groups about the yard and gate
His lifelong friends and neighbors wait;

On meadow lands that upward sweep
Move dairy cattle, grazing sheep;
From deep-loamed bottom fields, the sheen
Of gaily bannered corn is seen—
The square house, solid, painted white,
The barns and orchard at the right,
A restful, peaceful haven stands,
A monument to his dead hands—
The traffic sweeps along its way
Where once a swampy wood lot lay,
And as it passes, biting, quick,
A voice says, "Burying some hick!"

A wise man, he, among the wise,
Perceiving, through unjaundiced eyes,
Values that others could not see—
His hand found truth, unerringly;
Versed in craft little understood,
He knew the wild things of the wood,
The seasons, winds and winging birds
Familiarly as his own herds—
One with the earth, of God a part,
Washed clean of body, mind and heart,
He walked as only rulers can,
Asking no odds from life, or man—
The rubber sings, with muffled roar
The cars and trucks speed past the door
And leave a voice there, floating thin,
"Hey, look—some yokel has cashed in!"

A giant of the earth was he,
To win his fields from stone and tree,
To string his fences, hold each gain
Through searing drought and flooding rain;

Erecting his protective tents
Against the warring elements—
An ax, a saw, a grubbing hoe,
A furrow, then a greening row;
It took a giant, nothing less,
To wrest farms from the wilderness;
A lesser vision, strength and trust,
The elements would grind to dust—
His neighbors move about the place,
View, each in turn, his sleeping face—
A car slows, and a voice inside
Says, "Yeh, I guess some hayseed died!"

The man who breaks and tills the sod
Works in full partnership with God;
One single thought, plan matching plan,
The unity of God and man—
No finer tribute can be paid
To any dead than this; he made
A barren field to bloom, his hand
Brought fruitfulness unto the land.

—*Tramp Starr.*

251

OLD MEN

I love to sit with old men
Who never speak a word;
But seem to hear the silences
That I have never heard.

They sit and look with quiet eyes
As from an evening hill
That overlooks a valley which
The distance has struck still.

I love to sit with old men
Who never say a word:
I find I rise the quieter
For silences I've heard.
                              —*Robert Bell.*

252
THE GIFTS OF GOD

When God at first made Man,
Having a glass of blessings standing by;
Let us (said he) pour on him all we can:
Let the world's riches, which disperséd lie,
    Contract into a span.

So strength first made a way;
Then beauty flow'd, then wisdom, honor, pleasure:
When almost all was out, God made a stay,
Perceiving that alone, of all his treasure,
    Rest in the bottom lay.

For if I should (said he)
Bestow this jewel also on my creature,
He would adore my gifts instead of me,
And rest in Nature, not the God of Nature,
    So both should losers be.

Yet let him keep the rest,
But keep them with repining restlessness:
Let him be rich and weary, that at least,
If goodness lead him not, yet weariness
    May toss him to my breast.

                                    —*G. Herbert.*

253

A LAST WORD

Let us go hence: the night is now at hand;
    The day is overworn, the birds all flown;
    And we have reaped the crops the gods have sown;
Despair and death; deep darkness o'er the land,
Broods like an owl; we cannot understand
    Laughter or tears, for we have only known
    Surpassing vanity: vain things alone
Have driven our perverse and aimless band.

Les us go hence, somewhither strange and cold,
    To Hollow Lands where just men and unjust
    Find end of labour, where's rest for the old,
Freedom to all from love and fear and lust.
Twine our torn hands! O pray the earth enfold
Our life-sick hearts and turn them into dust.

                                    —*Ernest Dowson.*

INDEX OF AUTHORS

375

INDEX OF TITLES

INDEX OF FIRST LINES

Good-bye, proud world! I'm going home:, 248

To fight aloud is very brave, 170
To be, or not to be: that is the question:, 239
Trusty, dusky, vivid, true, 67
'Twas a balmy summer evening, and a goodly crowd was there, 91
'Twas good to live when all the range, 101
'Twas on a Friday morning, 105
'Twas on the shores that round our coast, 155

U

Underneath this myrtle shade, 87

V

Verse, a breeze 'mid blossoms straying, 232

W

Wal, no! I can't tell whar he lives, 95
We are not free; Freedom doth not consist, 172
"What is she making?" asked the mate;, 154
When all the world is young, lad, 225
When all this life is suddenly quite done, 212
When duty comes a-knocking at your gate, 196
When Father Time swings round his scythe, 86
When first my old, old love I knew, 34
When God at first made man, 252
When I remember all, 236
When, in disgrace with fortune and men's eyes, 42
When Spring, to woods and wastes around, 238
When the dust of the workshop is still, 231

When the Himalayan peasant meets the he-bear in his pride, 19
When things go wrong as they sometimes will, 180
When thou must home to shades of underground, 16
When trout swim down great Ormond street, 56
When you are tired of virtue, 38
"Where are you going tonight, tonight,—, 36
Whether I loved you who shall say?, 49
Which I wish to remark—, 117
While that the sun with his beams hot, 10
Who drives the horses of the sun, 141
Who will believe my verse in time to come, 42
Whoe'er she be, 6
Why so pale and wan, fond lover?, 29
With the leafy branches of the forest trees I lift my arms to pray, with the babbling brooks and singing birds I raise my voice in praise:, 205
Would I were one of those who preach no Cause—, 211

Y

Ye banks and braes o' bonnie Doon, 7
Yes, I've known the tragedy a desert life can give;, 138
Yet each man kills the thing he loves, 195
You may be ill and you may be sore, 182
You may sing your songs to the frozen North, 227
You to the left and I to the right, 133

INDEX OF THEMES

250